T0193115

Previous books by author:

The Trouble with Grace: a Study of its Multi-Dimensional Hebrew Root, kHesed. (On Kindle.)

The Hesed-Factor and the Parables of Jesus.

(At the Vineyard Bookstore, Evansville IN. 812-479-8777.)

Meditation Times with Elma

Navigating the Troubles Seas of Dementia: a Love Story

Keith Hueftle

WESTBOW
PRESS®
A DIVISION OF THOMAS NELSON
& ZONDERVAN

WestBow Press books may be ordered through booksellers or by contacting:

WestBow Press
A Division of Thomas Nelson & Zondervan
1663 Liberty Drive
Bloomington, IN 47403
www.westbowpress.com
844-714-3454

ISBN: 978-1-6642-3238-9 (sc)
ISBN: 978-1-6642-3237-2 (hc)
ISBN: 978-1-6642-3239-6 (e)

Library of Congress Control Number: 2021908354

Print information available on the last page.

WestBow Press rev. date: 05/27/2021

"…the content is so lovely and powerful and useful !…this is one of the best concrete examples of therapeutic grief-writing that I've had the privilege to read…The content is so lovely and powerful and useful…and I believe it will serve others."

— C. Ragsdale, Licensed Mental Health Counselor,

"It's the most beautiful love story… It has touched me deeply. I really wish it was a movie. I've never read something so painful but lovely…my heart aches."

— Genevieve McGuire, hospice chaplain.

"This book isn't just for those going through the Tsunami of dementia, but LIFE! What a testament…of sweet love between a husband and a wife. I have taken pictures with my smart phone of many various thoughts, passages, nuggets of wisdom and sent to friends and family to encourage them…."

—Lisa Kleinschmidt.

Dedicated

To the *anawim*—the little afflicted ones, unseen, out of sight, unremembered—in third world situations where they're driven from their homes; and to those who cost-fully care for their needs. To the afflicted all around us in the nursing homes, little lives, unseen, out of sight, unremembered. And to their caregivers, the nurses and CNAs and others who love *on-shift*. Then, especially to all those caregivers who find themselves in the unexpected role, the daunting task, of caring for a once young, once vital spouse—which can take them into depths of loving they never imagined.

Guide to the Themes

3 Finding Secure Currents In Christ Jesus 45

4 Longing For Release & Home 71

Introduction To An Oddysey . . .

INVISIBLE OLD PEOPLE

"Old people are invisible."

I never saw them. In a crowd, I'd maybe notice that pitiful old person for a moment, then shift my eyes away to something more engaging. "Old" was avoidable. Oh, of course, I had people-of-age who I knew personally, and that was different. They were real people, with a history; I knew something of their history, and I enjoyed engaging them. But apart from that, I avoided old people; they weren't interesting, they weren't vital.

Now I'm one of them. And they're all around me, because I'm in a home for seniors now. And besides the ones in the assisted living section with me, there are the others in the skilled-nursing unit where I regularly visit. There I see a category of what the Hebrew scriptures call *anawim*— "the afflicted ones." *Anawim* in scripture usually means the needy, the poor—the ones on the edge of society, not vital, not needed, but rather "needing"—the type of person on welfare, or homeless.

But I see the afflicted ones here, friends sitting, waiting—maybe engaged in Bingo, or lined up in their wheelchairs to go watch a concert, or maybe just waiting . . . to be taken to their room, or taken from their room. But waiting: some of them *years,* and still waiting. Many of these are not dementia patients, but just *old.* Some of them have people come to see them and take them out. Some of them seldom see anyone but the nurses and CNAs ("certified nursing assistants") and other patients. They're disremembered—by everyone but God, and (I should note) by some very loving and compassionate CNAs. Sometimes very funny, lively, and enjoyable CNAs.

Some of these minimum-wage CNAs—working two jobs to make a living—are "ministering angels", who *love!*

NEEDING TO LEARN TO "LOVE" . . .

We were once vital, and *noticed*. We were once young—and needing to learn to love . . . .

Elma was a foxy young brunette, her long mane of dark hair caught up in a French-braid at the back of her head. Just two years out of St. Andrews University in Scotland, with a degree in "Logic and Metaphysics"—she was formidable enough to scare away lesser young swains. She had just finished two years teaching in a little coalmining town outside of Edinburgh, riding the twenty miles there from Edinburgh on her Lambretta motor-scooter (with a few shin-scars on her knees to verify it). She'd just enrolled in probationary training in Glasgow—the Chicago of Scotland. Mornings she was taking the hour-long train there, to meet her young prostitute-clients and to counsel with judges.

At her parish in Edinburgh, I was the newly arrived pastor-in-training ("the American"). After a tumultuous, off-and-on romance, we were married, pregnant, and living in a little one-room bedroom apartment in the same massive, working-class parish. And I was discovering how formidable a new bride I'd married.

We were scheduled to move to America and had booked our ship's passage; but it was held up by a little matter—her being pregnant required getting doctor's approval. My little Scots wife, however, was stubbornly refusing to move on it; and I was getting impatient with her reluctance, afraid we might lose our passage. So, one evening I started to phone a doctor to get him to come to our flat (you could do that then). Elma was angry at my interfering—so angry that she threatened to be gone if the doctor showed up.

I was so frustrated I seriously thought of hitting her (a too common response of young husbands, with a too common pattern of abuse that follows if the woman acquiesces). Elma apparently saw it coming; for then and there, she let me know that if I ever did hit her, it would be the last I'd see of her.

I believed her and cooled off; and never again have I thought to hit.

(She did eventually get to a doctor—in her own time. And we did make it successfully to the ship . . . . and to America.)

I am forever grateful to this formidable little woman. She has proven not only strong but wise—willful, yes; but so am I. We've had many episodes of disagreement in our marriage—never physical, never hateful, but intense and (yes) hurtful. I would be stunned by her sharp rebukes. She was hurt by my bumbling insensitivities. We've many times had to learn to get over it—to take turns at initiating forgiveness and reconciliation. We've had *to learn to "love.*

I got too consumed with ministry. Affection waned. Loving needed to include learning the gift of *self-giving* love (biblically: *"aga-pe"*)—sacrificing interests for the other's good (Phil. 2:4)— sadly, for me a lesson long time in learning. But hugs, affection, talk, intimacy—though sometimes "on hold" for painful periods—they all continued important for both of us. All along. And in our latter, pre-dementia years we've delighted in declaring, in the presence of others, that: "We love each other madly!" (Silly maybe, but true.)

GIFTEDNESS GONE ?

Elma, besides being obviously bright, was funny, with an off-the-cuff humor.

She had the gift of organization. In Detroit, she took on a massive role with a co-op for young mothers (GDCNC, "Greater Detroit Co-op Nursery Council"), eventually organizing statewide and regional workshops.

While our children were growing, she taught adult-education classes in downtown Detroit: French, business English, and Shakespeare.

She had the gift of beauty and hospitality. She reveled in creating beautiful meals, not only for guests, but for family. On a very small budget (we had almost no new furniture) she made our home attractive and welcoming. Our house was center for many people coming and going. It was during the civil-rights movement of the 60s and 70s, and our place was home to interracial neighborhood friends, interracial leadership, and (two summers) as a boys' dorm for summer youth teams.

She was a gifted and clever public speaker. She gave talks for a women's three-day weekend and eventually coached the talks. She was invited to lead a young mothers' group for MOPS (Mothers of Pre-Schoolers). That involved regular instruction over a period of sixteen years, on childcare, husband-wife relationships, etc.—matters touching scores of young mothers.

Organization, articulateness, humor, beauty, hospitality, the mentoring of young women. Of these gifts, the first to go was "organization": the organization needed for thought, for meals, for baking. Eventually, the gift of "articulation;" that gift was gone, too.

The gifts of humor, and love of beauty, never left her.

A LONG LOOK AHEAD . . . .

As for that initial and difficult year, I have wonderful warm memories . . . of wonderful prayer times with Elma—even in some of the worst and scariest days.

On one particular day early on—in the midst of a confusing and tormented time for her—Elma prayed *for me* with such clarity and insight and wisdom that I kept wanting to stop her and somehow record it.

It was like a clear-flowing stream. As I watched—it was as though looking through a great, round picture-window watching a clear flowing stream go by . . . and realizing I was getting a chance to see what God had been doing in her in all that early, tumultuous time. It was a GIFT to me giving me assurance for some further scary times to come, knowing that God—behind the scenes and under cover—was doing a wonderful, maturing, finishing work in her . . .

. . . Just as He is doing a hidden finishing work *in me*—and in you as well—if we allow Him.

— O. Keith Hueftle.

Entering Unfamiliar Waters

It's been a classic odyssey these last years and months with Elma. Dementia, so ominous, so frightening, had taken us into the uncharted regions, the vicinities of old age, which nobody is ever prepared for. We had the benefit of hospice the last two years which afforded me some perspective I'd not otherwise have had. It was also the hospice chaplain and her urging that prompted me to even consider writing about these last times together.

When we checked out of the extreme unit where Elma had been cloistered for radical medication change, she'd gone in on foot. She'd come out *in wheelchair,* and visually shattered. The discharging nurse's last greeting was, "It'll get worse."

It had already been wrenching. Starting with the bit of memory loss, it had gone to episodes (lasting an hour and more) of sudden confusion and rage, triggered by nothing I could ever identify. It would take all that time, of pleading, reassuring, praying (crying to heaven for help), reassuring some more, calming, holding—and I suppose being visibly upset myself. For early on, after one of those occasions, Elma responded —having by then come out of it—and told me in her own marvelous, so calming, so loving way, "Keith, *dinnae greet, dinnae* be afraid" (in Scots: Don't cry; don't be afraid). "It's going to be all right." She was unbelievable—reassuring *me.* There were other occasions along the way where she would again astound me with her courage and wisdom and strength.

Early on, somewhat aware of what may be portending, Elma told me of her fear of not "getting to be like N_____ [one of her aunts]," who had gone into a long period of deep dementia until she no longer responded to family, voice, or touch. "I never want to go into a long dark tunnel like that." It was during one of our talks about the changes of old age we're experiencing that I talked to her in terms of "seasons." "Elma, we're in a

1

new season. We've never been *old* before. We don't know how to do it. We've got to learn to trust God in this time too. Every situation before, we've had to trust Him. Every new situation, we've had to learn to trust Him. Now again." And that became a theme.

The episodes continued for the next year and a half. Paranoia began to enter in, of people "traveling alongside" us, of people somewhere "upstairs in our home," to be taken care of, to be somehow catered for . . . "Catering" and overwhelming crowds waiting for hospitality were a part of her daytime nightmares those last months before The Break. Of the episodes, the most frightening occurred away from home—the really frightening ones, thankfully, when son or daughter was within reach and able to ride the storm with me until it was over.

The so-called "sun down" syndrome began a few months before the final break. It was another knot-in-the-stomach time; for those evenings became times when Elma wanted to leave me and was determined to "go live somewhere," or just to "go home." By then she was still driving.

But as this brief phase went on, it turned out to be for us a rather lovely and loving phase. As late afternoon would come, the restlessness would come on, and Elma would need to "catch a train." Or bus. To get away. To go home. So, as she would head for the car, I'd drop whatever I was doing and say to her, "Okay, but I'll go with you." We'd get in the car (I'd drive) and go to what have long been favorite spots for us: the riverfronts of downtown Evansville or Newburgh. We'd drive there, park and walk (if it was seasonal), find a bench, and watch the river, the clouds, the sunset, and a barge if there was one. Then, after a time of being quiet . . . content . . . we'd drive back home with no further incident.

For getaways—she *needed* getaways; she was bored. Reading was no longer interesting (she couldn't remember where she'd left off or what she'd last read). Groups had become a difficulty for her; she couldn't follow. For getaways, she'd begun driving herself to the Barnes and Noble bookstore to sit in the coffee shop. So, rather than letting her drive, I began dropping her off instead. I contacted the manager of the coffee shop, explained the situation, gave him my cell number, and asked him to phone me if there was any difficulty. Or I'd go there with her, as often as I could—for "a date." We'd order and sit together in the coffee shop. Cozy. Content. In love.

As for confusion and restlessness: there were two actual occasions where she began packing up and leaving. She was *leaving me*. An hour and a half it took . . . to dissuade, appeal, cajole. To get her to stay. To come to herself. On the second occasion, we had out-of-town friends who'd come impromptu for a visit and overnight stay. They were the grown children of schoolteacher friends from Detroit. During our time in the inner city there, Elma had offered to let these friends have a vacation while she took their kids for the week. "Mama Elma" she was to these four, now in their fifties. We'd had a great day with them—took them out to the Edgewater Café in Newburgh for lunch. It was a great time all day talking, catching up. But then, about seven o'clock that evening, Elma disappeared upstairs. When I went up to see about her, there she was, packing, determined to go—leaving me again to go find her home. When the friends became aware that something was not going well, they made a hasty, apologetic farewell and were on their way back to Georgia.

She never remembered the episodes. When they had passed, she was relieved, at peace, and ready to be loved and held.

The last week before The Break, I'd driven her to the bookstore myself. On my way back to pick her up, I was startled to spot her—across the street near Green River Road, and *walking*. It was mid-January and fortunately mild. But she was walking, heading home on her own—a two- or three-mile walk it would have been. (By God's goodness, I'd taken the same street as she had.) I did a U-turn and got her into the car. No incident. No upset.

That same evening—it was the last night she drove—she was in the car before I could intercept her. A worried hour later, I got a phone call from her. "Would you come and get me? I'm lost. I'm at some church. I stopped in here to use a phone." Totally unruffled she was. I was not so unruffled and had to figure out which church she'd be at. I went next door to the neighbor's for a ride. The neighbor unquestioningly drove me to the nearby church, which I hoped would be the one where I'd find her. There she was, waiting for us. No fear. No upset. Unabashed, she got into the car, and we went home to a peaceful night. But I took the keys from her that night and said I didn't want her driving anymore.

Two days later, we'd gone to Indy for a family weekend, where a grandson would be competing in a chess tournament. That night it happened. At midnight. She'd been up roving. I awoke to a scream. Sitting on the bathtub edge, she'd fallen backward into the tub. Her head was bleeding, her elbow broken. It was the first of many ambulance rides and of hours in ER.

It was the night of The Break.

As she was loaded into the ambulance, I yelled out to family, "*Pray for God's glory in all of this . . . !*" (I had no idea . . .)

From there, I knew we couldn't just go home. I'd need some place where I would have nursing help as her elbow healed. I booked a senior residence back home for a month so I'd have help with dressing and bathing her. Those were *mixed* days in which she had many moments of normalcy. But, though in elbow cast and needing the help I'd employed, she refused all help, whether with showers or dressing. She'd let no one else touch her. Nights were a madness, as she'd be wakeful, need help in the bathroom, and while there try to smash or tear apart the elbow cast.

It was a constant wakeful watch. And when *I didn't* watch (but slept), one of those nights—in the middle of the night—a new friend at the far end of the residence found Elma walking into her room half-clothed. This lady, gently, calmly walked Elma back to our room. She woke me, with explanations (and relief) that it was *into her room*, fortuitously, that Elma had come and not someone else's.

We had many friends stopping in to see us, eat with us, love us. But the restlessness exaggerated. Daytime or nighttime, Elma would begin to gather blankets or clothing and head down the long corridor to "pack the car" or "catch a bus" somewhere and *go*. After ten days, with me physically wiped out, the family intervened; a social worker came in to interview and make arrangements for the three-week period of "medication change" in a facility thirty miles away.

Elma was audience to the entire interview, hearing herself publicly discussed. Afterward, as our family walked ahead down the corridor, in trepidation at the thought of the ordeal they were in for—getting Elma into a car, driving her forty minutes away, and turning her over to lockup—Elma and I were walking behind. And as we followed, she was so amazing: with no thought for herself, but rather, speaking reassurance *to me* once again, "Keith, don't be afraid. It's going to be all right." And in transporting her to the facility, there was no to-do. No struggles. No horrific scene. She got into the car alongside me; and the two carsful of family headed off. (To her travail.)

Inside the facility, as they walked Elma away from us—to behind locked doors—I had only a little idea of what a torment it would be for her. Abandoned. No family member to accompany her to protect her. I heard that she fought, that they had had to sedate her, and no wonder: she had to be *touched/undressed by strangers*—even unknown male attendants. It was for her a Nazi concentration camp, a nightmare.

I traveled every day of the next three weeks to see her, for one hour plus: she in wheelchair, subdued, wilted. From there, it was a quick graduation to "permanent wheelchair."

In the next three months, there were six more medical facilities and three more ambulance rides. All of that, if you can imagine, when the thing most desired for persons in dementia is *"stability* and *security"*. . . .

The day after I brought her out and to a new facility, I myself had a pre-stroke episode and was hospitalized overnight. Friends insisted on my coming home with them. I not only did so but stayed several weeks; and in the next few months, I was repeatedly with them, a bed for me always available there. Such friends helped carry me in the subsequent three and a half years.

I began seeing Elma several times daily and for supper. Five months after admitting her to the final nursing facility ("The Home"), I was getting more crippled myself and variously in need of the supervision of assisted living. I signed into a section of Elma's facility—just down the hall and through double doors from her room. We had all our suppers together in her dining room, Sunday noon dinners as well. Every morning I brought her to our apartment in her wheelchair; then too, every afternoon and every evening until bedtime. We had "a three-room apartment," I told her—two rooms where we spent all our time, and one where she slept . . .

It's this period, three years of our Last Season, which began to hold a sweetness for us. It's those evenings, those bedtimes, when we shared the songs, the psalms, the stories, the talk, that made for the deep sharing times that I'm now calling *"Meditation Times with Elma."*

Navigating This Troubling Sea

Psalm 55: 4-6
My heart is in anguish

"My heart is in anguish within me;
the terrors of death have fallen on me.
Fear and trembling have beset me;
horror has overwhelmed me."

It's hard to keep up with what's happening. Everything is changing so drastically. So, if I'm having such a hard time with it, I can only guess at what Elma herself is thinking, feeling. She's so doped up! But from hearing things she's feared, and knowing how the disoriented moments come and go, I have a good idea of how daunting this experience is for her.

This Psalm 55 says it. (I read it with her.) *"My heart is in anguish within me . . . terrors . . . fear and trembling."* It's not only in the confusion of the many facility moves we've made, but also in the psychotic episodes when the UTIs have hit her.[1] . . . Is she thinking: What is happening to me? . . . and wondering at times: Where am I . . . Who are all these people around me? . . . Strangers . . . A welter of faces . . . some helping me do things . . . And does she then wonder: Why am I not doing them for myself . . . ?

She sees me. She almost always knows who I am and is so relieved to see me when I come. I'm a face she still knows and loves. I hold her. We talk. It is so good to talk. She talks to the others around her too. With some of them though, when they don't answer, is she wondering: Are they sick? . . . Am I sick too? . . . Am I in some kind of hospital? (She worked in a TB hospital one summer while in college.)

Only months later does she give voice to some of this.

---

[1] UTIs: "urinary tract infections." They raise havoc with the mind, especially for women. We wish we'd had a doctor's heads-up about this earlier.

She yields to the routine. Nurses give her medication. They help her to the bathroom. She goes to a dining room where we eat together evenings and Sunday noons . . .

She cries a lot when I'm gone.

Then, weeks into the time at The Home, she speaks plainly and says to me, "I'm afraid . . . I want to get out of here . . . How can I get out of here? . . . But where even could I go?"

And I read further to her from Psalm 55.

> *"Oh, that I had the wings of a dove. I would fly away and be at rest—I would flee far away and stay in the desert; I would hurry to my place of shelter, far from the tempest and storm.....I see violence and strife.....threats and lies never leave....."* (vv.6...11)

EARLY ON, CHECK FOR URINARY TRACT INFECTION

AS YOU PRAY FOR THEM, TRY TO SENSE WHAT THEY MAY BE EXPERENCING

Psalm 118:13-14
Pushed back, about to fall

> *"I was pushed back and about to fall,*
> *but the LORD helped me.*
> *The LORD is my strength*
> *and my song....."*

Portions of this psalm I read with Elma over and over through the months. It proved to be a kind of touchstone through the months, and as much for *me* as it was for her.

This Psalm 118 is so good that I asked family to memorize it. From verse 1 right on through, it's got everything a young believer will need for the fight. First, as bottom-line, it embraces the fact that ***"God is good,"*** underscored by His **blood-sworn pledge to save us**—a 4-fold forever-promise—and the determined assertion of **His Presence** with us as we enter in to the inevitable battle of the life of a believer. From there, a whole sequence of helps . . .

(As I read it with Elma): So much is happening with us. And this psalm says it for us. It reckons with heavy things—scary things—that come upon us, and with moments like these when we're yelling inside, *"HELP! I'm pushed back and about to fall . . . . !"*

And, over and over as we cry out for Him—He does: He *helps* us. And we find ourselves able to say—once, and then over and over—the same blessed confession, *"You, Lord, are my Strength and my Song!* And you absolutely have come to be *my Salvation!* (What would we ever do without you . . . ?)"

That first year was so hard, the year after The Break. When Elma came back from lock-up, she was so demolished. She looked terrible, her face unlike her. She could still feed herself at first and get to the bathroom with help. But there were more falls, more ambulance rides to ER. Within weeks the wheelchair became the mandatory mode for getting around.

We were in a fourth facility, then a fifth and a sixth. Poor decisions from admissions at one facility led them to demand that I provide 24-hour care in the facility (would you believe!) —*two days after they had pre-approved her!*

But that meant an additional outlay of $12,000 a month! So—until I was able to have our doctor get Elma out of there and into an *interim* facility—for much of the two-more-weeks there, *I was* "the 24-hour care." Needless to say, I was exhausted. "My stomach is knotted up, Lord, with fear of all that I can't ensure for her". . . .

I don't know how well I prayed with Elma on those days. All I know is that I had permission from the facility to be in bed with her those nights, so as to comfort and secure her (our queen-sized bed was in her room yet at that point), as well as to help in the middle-of-the-night visits to the bathroom.

It was from there to the interim facility, then—another three weeks later—to the nursing home (The Home) where we finally, providentially landed. Even there though, at that final facility—*after just two weeks*—a visiting psychiatrist was arranging for Elma to be sent back to the lock-up facility "for further meds-adjustment!" I hit the ceiling and stopped it. Talk about "a secure, stable environment for dementia patients!" That episode left me certain that nothing had changed: I had still to be on guard for her constantly.

I exalt you, Lord, you lifted us out of the depths...I called to you for help... you brought us up from She-ol and spared us from going down into the Pit. You rescued us, because you delighted in us. Glory and praise to you . . .

PROVIDE THEM ALL THE STABILITY POSSIBLE

Psalm 31:2-3
My rock and my fortress

*"...be my rock of refuge, a strong fortress to save me.
Since you are my rock and my fortress,
for the sake of your name, lead and guide me."*

Initially—before moving into The Home with Elma—my visits with her, though frequent, were so scrambled by circumstances that I don't remember the content of our talk times together. But I remember my own prayer at the time, focused on such as this psalm. It was a cry for help.

I was with Elma so constantly. And I wanted to be. More than anything, I didn't want her to feel abandoned. But it all was overwhelming. My planner in those early months was jammed daily with phone calls, arrangements to make, ways to look out for Elma's welfare.

I was her needed advocate. She'd always told me, "If anyone ever goes to hospital, they need someone with them as advocate." She was right. There were so many things to do to guard her. And I had to stay well, to stay alive, for her sake.

As I read this scripture with her, it became as much for my sake as it was for hers, part of my arsenal. I needed God as Rock and Fortress, my steadier, my protection, against all kinds of things assailing me. I badly needed my own times of prayer and waiting on the Lord.

I needed His leading. Daily, mornings before breakfast, nightly on my knees before climbing into bed, I was forever asking Him, "Help me to love her *well*, to love her *wisely.*"

Father, you're my lifeline. You're my Life. I ask you to let me hear you well so that I can hear Elma well. Help me know what she needs, and daily the right scripture and song or word for her.

Always, it's for your Name's sake that I ask. For I know that your Name is at stake in all these things we do here—your glory.

So, glory to you, who sit on the Throne—and unto the Lamb. Blessing and honor, and glory and power, forever and ever!

YOU YOURSELF: GET CLOSE TO YOUR ROCK

YOU'RE GOING TO NEED A LOT OF FORTIFICATION

Psalm 30: 6 -7
When you hid your face

"When I felt secure, I said, 'I will never be shaken';
LORD, when you favored me,
you made my royal mountain stand firm;
but when you hid your face, I was dismayed . . ."

"*When I felt secure . . .*" In one of the early times, as I read this psalm with Elma and verbalized that particular line, a clear "mm-hmm" of agreement came from her. (Talk already had begun to fail for her.)

(In talking with Elma): Oh, it's so like all of us when we feel great in life, when we think we're in control, so secure, so confident. You know about feeling self-assured . . .

But we're in a new time now. We're in a new season. All this is new now. We've never learned how to "do Old" (trying to be funny about it).

So, we've got to learn to trust God all over again. As in every new situation before, we've had to trust Him. This time too. For this is new to us, and we've got to learn to trust Him again.

We need to remember, this is not new for God. It's new for us, but not for Him. He's had people in this situation before. He's carried thousands of others like us through this. And He's carrying us now.

As always, I sing with her one of our evening hymns we used to sing at home. Then our prayer time.

Praise you, our Father. We bless you that you know our frame; you remember that we're dust. But help us: it's so hard for us, and so unwelcome.

We cry out to you, Our God. Hear our voice. Turn our mourning into dancing that our hearts may sing to you and not be silent.

HELP THEM EMBRACE A NEW SEASON

Psalm 32:10
Surrounded by saving love

"Many are the woes of the wicked,
But the LORD's unfailing love[2]
surrounds the one who trusts in him."

Even after she was in The Home, it was so frustrating. I'd often come and find her slumped over in her chair. Even awake, she'd be atilt, pillows pushed under one side to get her up half straight. We didn't realize it at first; but, through all those months—who knew how long?—UTI's had been decimating her.

Though she was still talking then, and mostly cogent, she was often

---

[2] *khesed,* the Hebrew word for the Near Eastern practice of a radical "hospitality" in which one commits his life for the protection and provision of whoever comes into his tent. It became the word for God's *blood-sworn, commitment of saving help* for us, bloodily demonstrated in His Son's self-giving act for us.

out of her head, manic. She patrolled the corridors in her wheelchair, up and down, back and forth, "polishing the floors to keep them shiny," she told us. At one point, lasting several weeks, they had her reclined—flat out in her wheelchair (I never knew why); but she was propelling herself backwards in the corridor and slamming herself into the wall.

We heard they were making many drug-changes; but it was impossible to discuss it with the doctor assigned to her, for we could never get an appointment with him. Finally, with a new doctor, we were able to deal with the UTIs, and Elma was able to become a little more recognizably herself.

After I myself moved into The Home—on the scene and with her medications leveled out—life began to take on something like normalcy. Initially, though, when I brought Elma to our apartment, she fought coming into it. She physically resisted going through the door saying, "This isn't the right place." (I had to laugh.) So, once getting her inside, I introduced her to it, announcing, "This is now *our new apartment*."

(Our talk time): The psalm says, "the Lord's blood sworn commitment to help surrounds those who trust in Him." It's surrounding us, Elma. And not only that, but His saving, intervening love has been at work arranging all this for us.

Look at it. We get to be under the same roof together now . . . Here in our apartment, I can give you snacks, and read to you . . . You can nap; I can nap . . . We'll get to play music and talk, and have our little kisses . . . And all of this daily while I work on the computer, or make my phone calls . . . It's as close to being home as we can get. Elma, we're so lucky, so blessed. It says, "The Lord's saving love *surrounds* those who trust in Him." Jesus talks about moving mountains. Well, His sworn Saving Love is a *moving force* for those who trust Him, and It has been working good things for us.

Back in her room for bedtime—a tight little room with double-occupancy and a divider-curtain—we close the day together. There's a little scripture bit I've picked, and always one of our evening hymns, then our night prayers—and, of course, the face-hugs. (Since body-hugs are now so impossible, we still get to have lots of "face-hugs"—with all our little kisses slipped in. All that, so important!)

> *Underneath are the Everlasting Arms. O Lord, you lifted us*
> *up when we were falling. You hear our cry and save us.*
>
> *Thanks, Lord, for surrounding us with your saving love.*
>
> *Guard over Elma's heart and mind this night, in Christ Jesus. Give*
> *her sweet peace, and joy in the morning. (Face-Hug, and kiss.)*

HELP THEM TO EXPERIENCE SOME NORMALCY

Psalm 34:7-10
"The Angel of The LORD"

> *"The angel of the LORD encamps around those who fear him*
> *and he delivers them....*
> *The lions may grow weak and hungry,*
> *but those who seek the LORD*
> *lack no good thing."*

In the first few days at The Home, we had discovered the patio. It was just outside the nursing dining room. We found that we were able to have some of our meals there.

Our first two summers were amazingly non-humid for Evansville, so we were able to have our suppers out every evening but four, for heat—amazing! It was such a haven, a respite, from the institutional grind. Even in months to come, when Elma was largely unresponsive, the sights and feel of the out-of-doors were enough to bring from her little exclamations of delight.

There on the patio, if she weren't sleeping, we'd read stories of northern England and the young Scottish veterinarian just starting his practice there. When the family came to visit, they'd also read these and other stories with her. There'd be obvious enjoyment and sometimes comment from her as we'd read.

(Talking with her about the scripture): Look at us—on The Patio! We've been rescued from "our prison" and get to escape into the beauty of this open space! It almost doesn't seem fair, we're so blessed. We get to sit out here where it's all quiet—under the canopy of the sky, engulfed by these massive, aged trees—to watch the clouds, the vapor trails and all, as we used to do at the riverfronts. It's a bit of *normalcy.*

The CNAs[3] are wonderful. They are so congenial, so solicitous in bringing our supper trays here. (They're funny: they say it gives them an excuse for a little break outdoors themselves . . .)

And we get to be together . . .

O praise you, our Father. It's right: "we lack no good thing." It's amazing how you're taking care of us Even this Evansville summer is so amazing: we've gotten to eat outdoors almost every night. Thanks for the beauty of your world, and that we get to enjoy it together.

TAKE ADVANTAGE OF ANY BREAK FROM THE ROUTINE TO HELP TO FILL THEIR MOMENTS

Luke 11:5-8
The Midnight Visitor

"...'a friend of mine on a journey has come to me,
and I have no food to offer him.'
....yet because of your shameless audacity
[the Neighbor] will surely get up
and give you as much as you need . . ."

I talked over this parable with Elma—but only later.

What I didn't tell her was that, in having her in my care, I saw myself as the man in this parable, unable to supply any of the needs of his overnight guest—a desperate and frantic situation. For, to take in a guest in that culture, meant the obligation to protect and provide for a guest—over and

---

[3] CNA: certified nursing associates, the official title for "aides."

above the safety and needs of one's own family! An obligation touching all the houses in the village along with him.

As in this parable, I saw Elma as my "midnight friend," one whose deepest needs were such that I had nothing that could supply them. My "cupboard" was effectively *bare*. I knew that I could love her and meet some of the *human needs*. But the essential matters of peace, security—and the protection of her spirit—those were things I couldn't provide.

But I knew where to go to find them: next door at the house of Covenant God who is committed to Kingdom essentials—"if met with confident, persistent knocking," says Jesus.

So, night prayer times in my own apartment became the time for outsourcing on such matters. Confident it was a Kingdom-essential in God's mind, I pounded and pounded on the door of this next-door, Neighbor God. And I found that He, indeed, was ready with all those needed essentials. In the days and months ahead, as over and over I prayed thus for her needs, gratefully, I found Him providing them all: peace, security and the treasured presence of His Holy Spirit.

I praise you, Savior, for giving her the very things I cannot give her: contentment, security, trust and peace. Let her soul find refuge in you, Lord Jesus. Let her soul cling to you.

O God, faithful covenant-keeping God, who sits upon the throne and unto The Lamb, be blessing and honor and glory and power forever, Amen!

KNOW YOU'RE OVER YOUR HEAD. THERE IS SO MUCH YOU CANNOT DO FOR THE ONE YOU LOVE

Psalm 42:4-6
Among the festive throng

"I remember . . . how I used to go to the house of God,
under the protection of the Mighty One
with shouts of joy and praise
among the festive throng.
Why, my soul, are you downcast?
Why so disturbed within me?
Put your hope in God, for I will yet praise him,
my Savior and my God."

(With Elma. I sing it with her, as a song we often sang from the Scottish Psalter in Scotland) *"Why art thou then cast down, my soul? What should discourage thee? And why with vexing thoughts art thou disquieted in me?"* It's a favorite song we've long sung. It's from Psalm 42, of course; and it's worth recalling, because it not only bewails these troubling seas that threaten to overwhelm us: *"All your waves and breakers have swept over me"* (v.7); but it reminds us of the throngs of friends which we've known through community, both in Scotland and Detroit.

And look how many friends have come to see us while we're here! (*Do we realize how important friends are . . .?*)

We're surrounded with them and their love. A couple drove in from Atlanta during the crux-time, the 24-hour-a-day marathon at the one facility. They spent a day with us, played music and sang with us, honored Elma's need for rest and prayed with me about "resting in the Lord." The conversations—and the break—were for me a great refreshment.

Within the next year women friends from all over came to see Elma: Los Angeles, Chicago, Minneapolis, Virginia, Carolina, Indy. Elma always knew all of them. But within that year she also lost the ability *to talk to* almost all of them.

Gratefully, friends continued to come to see me/us, often in our apartment. Whether Elma was asleep or awake, I'd bring her wheelchair out and into the midst of the friends. If she was awake, she listened very intently to the discussion, and on occasion contributed a comment or an assent. The participation was intensely stimulating for her. Elma loved it—it's like old times, excepting in old times she'd have been right in the mix with her own sage comments and witticisms.

Father, it is so great to have these friends here. How did you know to do that! You have such great ideas! Thanks for these people; thanks for putting us in life where we can love so much and be loved so much.

Guard over them as they come and go and guard over the purposes you have for each of them themselves.

LET FRIENDS KNOW THE IMPORTANCE OF INCLUDING THIS LOVED ONE IN THE TALK TIMES

RELISH THOSE FRIENDSHIPS. LEAN ON THEM. WELCOME THEM.

Psalm 63:1...8
My soul clings to you

*"...I thirst for you, my whole being longs for you,
in a dry and parched land where there is no water.
....Because your love is better than life,
my lips will glorify you...
I cling to you; your right hand upholds me."*

She'd been through so much: the midnight fall, with broken elbow and cast; the UTIs that brought such confusion (its seriousness none of us aware of), the twenty-one days in lock-up, abandoned, left to fight strangers with needles and who-knows-what intentions . . .

I didn't want her to experience abandonment any further. There was need for her to be held and hugged—like when I'd gotten permission from the charge nurses to crawl into bed with her in those earlier times at The Home.

Presence, constancy.

Mornings after breakfast, she'd come with me. She had a tilt-down wheelchair by then. I'd park her either beside me as one or both of us would have the life-giving nap; or I'd park her just at my elbow while I'd work at the computer. Only rarely did she want to watch television. If she was awake and talking, I'd stop and listen.

By then I was logging each day's mood and responses, capturing each word I could get. We'd have music from the nearby old stereo: classics— we both loved Dvorak and Smetana's *Moldau*—and bluegrass, and CDs of our son Ben's Wolfgang Orchestra. With the bluegrass (on days when I had enough energy and my feet worked), we'd "dance"—I'd take both hands and we'd *move! Jitterbug*. Shoulders weaving, make-believe whirls. Delight. Fun. We loved it.

By nighttime we'd have the twenty- to sixty-minute bedtimes. This particular psalm, along with other psalms and songs I'd memorized, became the basis for our nightly meditation times and for our prayer.

(Talk time with Elma): It's such a relief to get to be in the same place with you, just down the hall, and through the double doors (a situation I would reiterate for her frequently). To have you with me in the apartment every day, supper with you every night, Sunday dinner. To have the bedtime with you, the songs and scripture.

This psalm is becoming our "signature psalm." It sings our absolute need for our Father, the Holy One of Israel—as for food and drink. Desperate. And it acknowledges those sweet and precious times when *we ourselves* have known His presence—and then confesses a rare discovery: that this sworn, loving, saving-presence [*ᵏhesed*]⁴ is *better than life* itself. Such a rare and awed discovery—we'll want to praise Him forever. And to lift our hands in utter adoration.

Even on our beds, and as darkness falls, you can remember how He's caring for and has helped us. And it ends with that strong affirmation that—even as my soul would want to *cling* to this Most High God and

---

⁴ From first, being a commitment of the radical hospitality, *khesed* became the central, sworn-covenant word of the Old Testament, the word the LORD God used to bind Himself in family-partnership with a whole people. Far stronger than "mercy" (as usually translated), **there is thus good reason for God's People to prefer it over life itself.**

Savior (feeble as my own hold is)—He *holds me . . . grasps me . . . securely . . .*
with a grasp[5] that will not let go of us.

> *I praise you, God our Father, for never leaving us or forsaking*
> *us. O, God our God, you are our God: our souls thirst for you,*
> *our flesh longs for you, as in a dry and weary land. I praise you*
> *that your costly Saving Love is better than life itself. And that*
> *your hold on us, your grasp of us, is stronger than Death.*

> *Thank you, Savior God! Let her soul find refuge in you. Let*
> *her soul cling to you as you hold and grasp her securely!*

DO ALL YOU CAN TO LET THEM KNOW THAT THEY ARE NOT ABANDONED

MONITOR THEIR TV, WATCHING SO THAT THEIR SOLITARY TIME IS NOT DOMINATED BY CYNICAL UGLINESS

---

[5] From the Hebrew root, **tamakah**, meaning "lay hold of; grasp; hold fast." Brown,
Driver, & Briggs, op. *cit.*, p. 1069.

Psalm 30: 7-9
Dust doesn't praise you

"…when you hid your face, I was dismayed.
To you, LORD, I called; to the Lord I cried for mercy:[6]
What is gained if I am silenced,
If I go down to the pit?
Will the dust praise you?
Will it proclaim your faithfulness?"

(Talk during a plateau time, late autumn): We both know the feeling of thinking we're unshakeable. We've had those times. But then comes the moment when the whole world falls apart. We've had a few of those . . . Detroit, when we felt all alone in that inner-city situation . . . then when we moved to southern Indiana despite all the red flags . . . and when you were fighting that one particular fight of your life.

Apart from that, you've pretty well toughed your way through everything. Undaunted. Confident. Strong. All the way from facing the school-ground bully, to handling the "borstal girls"[7] in Glasgow; and the Lamaze-birthing of our three children—the last of which we nearly had to self-deliver during the Detroit uprising. To watching the ER medic stitch up your forearm, long after the medication had worn off . . . watched it, unflinching, uncomplaining (while watching, I evinced enough anguish for us both).

This psalm echoes a confidence in the God of our salvation by a person in a time of The Dark Night of the Soul, determined to believe that staying in this rotten position is not going to please or glorify God one bit. So, he challenges God for Who He is in the confidence that even though he is in the pit, God won't let him stay there.

---

[6] I often used the Hebrew names **Yahveh** and **Adonai** with Elma in our talks. **Yah-veh** *and* **YAH** (a shortened form for **Yahveh** often used in the Hebrew Psalms, occasionally in the prophets) are God's actual name. Though often **un**pronounced out of reverence for the holy Name, "**YAH,**" as a shortened form is pronounced over and over again, as in the praise expression: "*HalleluYAH.*"

[7] "Borstal" girls or boys, in Britain, were young people who had come under the rule of the court system. Elma, as a probation officer, was in charge of a caseload of 13/14-year old girls (prostitutes, and other such offenses), and had to oversee a day camp full of them one summer.

Elma, where we are now is never a place we thought we'd be. It's hard. We're at the mercy of old age and all its pitiable conditions. Who ever thought it could be like this? But God is a faithful God. He knows the dust doesn't praise Him. Dust won't proclaim His faithfulness . . . But we can . . . and we do. He hears our cry for help, and we're going to be able to say (as the Psalm continues, verses 11 and 12):

"You turned my wailing into dancing; you removed my sack-cloth and clothed me with joy, that my heart may sing to you and not be silent. O Lord my God, we will give you thanks forever!" Give us good night's sleep this night. Wake us up in the joy of our salvation. (Face-hug, and a kiss.)

HELP THEM TO KNOW THAT—IN THIS NEW AND UNWELCOME SITUATION—THEY CAN REACH OUT IN TRUST AS THEY'VE DONE BEFORE

John 14:11...20
"The Passage"

*"Believe me when I say that I am in the Father
and the Father is in me....
On that day you will realize
that I am in my Father,
and you are in me
and I am in you."*

With the UTIs under control, and times of clarity, Elma was chatty. She cheered on the patients as they played balloon volleyball—even though she chose not to participate; and she enjoyed speaking French to the African aide. She always knew every friend who came to visit her, even later on when she could scarcely speak.

But as that first December wound down, moods too were daily up and down. She was crying much; and in one very serious moment at bedtime she prayed: "I want to go Home soon." Along with it and in so many words, she asked that things would be "in order," and then also, that "the passage would be *short.*"

As if to help along an answer to her own prayer, in the following weeks she began to stop eating. As a result, she was eventually transitioned to the section of the dining room where CNAs fed you. By then, she was also sleeping much of the time; and her communication ability was lessening. She was talking lots still, but it came out in phrases that didn't connect, or were just unintelligible. (As I recorded our daily times together in my notebook, I'd write "ttt", meaning "trying to talk.")

With the change of doctors, he'd suggested taking her off the high levels of psychotic medication. As a result, she had become more responsive, alert, and—along with it—probably more aware of her circumstances. Hence, more crying.

(In our talk time): "The Passage"—leaving here—is a scary thought, I know. For all of us. But we have so many words to assure us: Jesus' own promises, that he's *prepared a place for us . . . . that he'll come back and take us to be with him . . . . that we'll realize that we are in him and he's in us . . .*

He's already wrapped those who love him in himself. For a long time now, saints have recognized that we're "enveloped/wrapped!" in the Lord Jesus. It's too awesome, too mysterious a thing, to picture. So, passage to the other side involves us *being carried:* carried in Jesus himself, who is Lord of Heaven and Earth—Lord of both sides.

We're *swathed* in him, even now, until the Day when he's ready to present us like newborns to the Father.

Help us, Father, to know the deep things of our abiding, of our being carried by you. Of our being wrapped in your Son, swaddled in him, secured by him. Give us good sleep this night, and wake us in the joy of our salvation.

Praise, honor, and glory to you Who Live Forever!

THERE ARE TIMES OF TRANSITION, UPS AND DOWNS, BUT IT'S NOT NECESSARILY THE END

Romans 8:28-29
Conformed to the First-Born

"…in all things God works for the good
of those who love him,
who have been called according to his purpose.
For those whom God foreknew
he also predestined to be conformed
to the likeness of his Son,
*that he might be the **first-born**[8]*
among many brothers and sisters."

It's the second half of this scripture that is bottom-line for me, and it's one I tell myself. With Elma I reviewed it from various angles over the months. It speaks "the purpose," which the otherwise favorite verse, Romans 8:28, only alludes to, namely, that God fully but painfully intends *to make us like* His Son.

(Our talk time together): God still has work that He's doing in us—even in old age. There is a maturing and refining to happen in us. For there is a lot of *ugliness* in us each (as I say it pointing at myself, grinning but serious), ugliness that needs to get worked *out*.

But the wonder of it is we're *pre-appointed* to be like the "first-born." Elma, it's so amazing. We're to look like JESUS in the Father's eyes—He so proud of what we've become. And so it is, that on the way some of the old junk in us has to die! And that's okay, isn't it?. . . because we couldn't take any of that old stuff into Forever with us. We *couldn't!*—it wouldn't fit, and we wouldn't be recognizable as *family.*

So, there's some hard stuff to put up with in the meantime—O yes, isn't it though?—while God gets rid of it.

And, on the way there, Elma, (I was able to tell her in subsequent days), *God has been doing a thing in you* . . . there's a beauty, a maturing in you. A refining . . . *Look at you!* We're going to have the family-likeness! And both of us to be *recognizable—as FAMILY!*

---

[8] My emphasis.

Thanks, Father. Thanks for the unbelievable design you've had in mind for us. What you've already done in us, and what you're doing yet.

O Lord our God, it's our desire—we've said it to you so often before, and we say again: we want to praise you as long as we have life and breath. And then—forevermore.

OVER AND OVER AFFIRM THAT THIS SEASON IS NOT WASTED BUT THAT—ALL THE WHILE—OUR GOD IS DOING WONDERFUL, IMPORTANT THINGS IN IT

SONG:
"Sweet Chariot"

"I looked over Jordan and what did I see,
Comin' for to carry me home?
A band of angels comin' after me. . .
Comin' for to carry me home."[9]

Within a year, Elma had deteriorated so much that we were urged by nursing to connect with hospice. On a subsequent day the doctor was speaking with us about it.

Elma who was present—but until then appeared to be a silent observer—interjected her own assent: "IT'S TIME FOR SOME DECISIONS," she said. Startled, I turned to look at her and was delighted to see a huge, self-pleased smile!

Soon after then, coached by Genevieve the hospice chaplain, instructions "for releasing Elma" began—our family along with me—instructions for *letting go of her,* and for coming to terms with such a readiness.

(Talk time with Elma) There we were, in that session with the chaplain; and I was telling her about the funeral services that I'd already planned

---

[9] Traditional Spiritual, public domain.

for us each, and that you and I had talked about the plans. As I was describing the upbeat, victorious elements in the service for her, I looked over, surprised and delighted, to see you beaming with approval! And you know how glad that made me . . . .

I often sang with her. And I loved the strength and the simplicity of the spirituals. So, at bedtimes—or during the day, in our apartment, depending on her mood—I'd sometimes sing "Sweet Chariot" (that song among many) about a chariot coming to carry us home. I began to picture various ways for her in which the transition would happen: not as a dark tunnel to go through as she had feared, but "being carried"—Jesus himself personally, carrying us the last distance. Holding us securely.

O Lord Jesus, Son of the Father, because you have helped us, we SING!— under the shadow of your wings we sing. Our souls cling to you, and with your own strong right hand, you hold and grasp us securely.

SONGS CAN BE A HELP.

HELP THEM BEGIN TO PREPARE FOR THE TRANSITION, OPENLY TALKING ABOUT IT.

Revelation 5:13
The Lamb of God

"To him who sits on the throne and to the Lamb be praise and honor and glory and power, for ever and ever!"

I'd been holding her and talking with her in terms of "The Lamb of God": of our long honoring of Him and His work. And of our own work all these years—good work, blest work, work offered up—but that the work needing *to be done **for us** is done!* Not only that it is *done for us* (and on our behalf), but that it *is FINISHED.*

Of all Elma's speech that evening, none of it was understandable. The only cogent speech that evening was her repeating—of all that I was saying to her—"THE WORK IS DONE."

(Our talk time) You have long had a special regard for Jesus as Lamb of God. A special reverence for him in that capacity as "having been *slain for us.*" Almost always, in situations where we felt the freedom to do so—when a song acknowledging The Lamb was sung—you'd rise to your feet, much as when in Britain the people come to their feet in the presence of the king or the queen.

It is such an awesome thing to regard that the One Who is Forever and Ever would come into our sorry and sinful domain, join the little ones who are afflicted and distressed, and himself take on our sorry estate.

Awesome too to know that his blood is effective for every "tribe and tongue and people and nation." That it applies to the domains where *honor* is paramount—as in the Islamic world; and where *power* is revered—as in the communist blocs; and where *glory* is coveted—as in the video-worshipping capitalistic world. And too, where *blessing* is recognized and esteemed—as in the people of Israel.

> *Worthy is the Lamb, who was slain, to receive power and riches and wisdom and strength, and honor and glory and blessing!....*
>
> *[For] with your blood you purchased for God from every tribe and tongue and people and nation and made them to be a Kingdom and Priests to serve our God, and they will reign on the earth.*

(Revelation 5:13, then 9-10)

HELP THEM REACH FOR THE TRANSCENDENT, FOR THE GLORY AND WONDER WAY BEYOND US, WAY BEYOND NOW.

Psalm 32:8-9
I will instruct you

"I will instruct you and teach you in the way you should go.
I will counsel you with my loving eye on you.
Do not be like the horse or mule
which have no understanding
but must be controlled by bit and bridle
or they will not come to you . . ."

It was well into that second year, when we were out for a walk in the sunshine, Elma in her wheelchair, and I, hobbling a bit badly by then. We were just outside the building's south entrance with full view of it and the wing of Elma's nursing section. We'd stopped for a needed sit-down for me. Bright and cheerful, Elma suddenly looked up and asked the full, searching question: "HOW DID I HAPPEN TO COME TO THIS PLACE?" (That was a stunner, considering she hadn't said much for a while.)

I answered as simply and truthfully as I could muster, "You had a fall. You broke your elbow and split the back of your head. So, we needed a place to help take care of us, and that's how we've ended up here."

She wanted to understand her circumstances. How we got where we are, but also to countenance *what was happening.*

(In my talk with her): The Father Himself so greatly desires to have us understand what He's doing, and to be open to that, so that we can work along with Him in what He's doing in us. Memorized scripture is so helpful for that. Knowledge of His promises, so critical. Understanding of His long-term purposes for us, starting here-on-earth.

More than anything, the Father wants us *near*—in a close . . . tight . . . intimate relationship with Him—not to be forever like some wild, rebellious thing, an untamed animal who rears and reels away at any approach of his would-be master. He wants the beginning of that closeness even now, in preparation for the eventual, marvelous, glorious closeness which He has prepared for all of us . . . from before the beginning *of space-time . . . .*

O Lord, we want to come near you. Don't let us continue like a
horse or mule with no understanding. Help us to trust you now.

Instruct us and teach us so we'll have confidence in what you're doing with us. And we do long, *so desperately, to be near YOU.*

Thanks, that that's your own heart's desire for us in Christ Jesus.

HELP THEM TO UNDERSTAND THEIR CIRCUMSTANCES, AND ALSO GOD'S CLOSENESS TO US IN ALL OF IT

Psalm 119:64.
Full of your saving love

"The earth is filled with your love, LORD."

In that first year and a half, I was able to get Elma out and into our car to go on little drives, even to go out to eat, and to get to church. It meant negotiating her out of the wheelchair, into and out of car, the restaurant, the pew; and it meant me getting the wheelchair in and out of the trunk of the car. A difficulty, but it was worth it. A bit of normalcy.

It was so great, getting to meet friends at restaurants. At church, people were helpful getting us in and out of the car and wheelchair. And for a short duration at church, I relished seeing Elma able yet to sidle in and out of the pew, still to stand and sing hymns alongside me.

But increasingly all this required the help of staff persons from The Home to negotiate her in and out of the car. So, as the months went on— by the end of that year—she began to lose her ability to help, to stand, to pivot. It got to be too much for staff; and the rides and the outings all had to come to a stop.

(Our talk time) And here in this life we get to learn to love . . . All the little ways in which we get to love each other. (Why does it take so long to learn it? . . .) We're surrounded by the saving love of God, working for us in every event of every day. And in every event of those days, Elma, I *get to love you*. I'm so lucky.

The best thing in all my life has been just that: all of these years of my getting to know and love you.

Every day, a love song is in my head. There are five or six of them, and every day one comes into my mind, my heart: of my love for you . . .

Father, thank you. What a plan you've had, for human beings to get past themselves and able to love someone more than themselves. Your plan. Your kind of love.

IN ALL THE CHANGES, LET THEM KNOW OVER AND OVER, IN EVERY WAY POSSIBLE, HOW YOU CHERISH THEM, HOW YOU LOVE THEM

Weathering Losses
Limitations Frustrations

SONG:
Nobody knows . . . but JESUS!

"Nobody knows the troubles I see.
Nobody knows, but Jesus.
Nobody knows the troubles I see.
Glory, Hallelujah!"[10]

In the first year at the facility, Elma would often be found crying. All those times it was hard to know how to console her. (*"Don't jolly me!"* she'd always told me.) I'd long since heard from her the grating effect of someone who is *too happy too early in the morning*, when the other person is slow waking up. I was glad to discover it early in our marriage—reminded by her, of course—and to wise up. A proverb too says it aptly, in effect that: if you bless your neighbor too loudly, too early in the morning, *"it will be taken as a curse."* (Proverbs 27:14)

We had often joked about "losing *parts.*" (Sorry for the old-age humor.) Mornings, while still in our last house, we might greet each other with, "Hi. How's all your parts?" Or sometimes, "Lose any parts overnight?" So then sometimes at The Home, to take a lighter note, I'd quip about my *own* parts dropping off. Feet and ankles. Hearing. Sight. Voice—many nights I could no longer sing with her, my voice so gone. And more. (Never mind; you don't need to know "the more.")

But when those despondent times hit her, I reached for the same note as sounded in the Spirituals. It often had a consoling effect. It helps to know that you're understood when you're down and can't explain why

---

[10] Traditional spiritual, public domain.

you're down. So, I'd sing to her, and talk about it as I sang. It may be extremely corny, but here's how it went.

"*Sometimes I'm up, sometimes I'm down. Oh, yes*"—*don't you know it*—*Lord?* (And I'd *ad lib* about what's happening as I sang—the situation, the difficulties, the frustrations.) "*Sometimes I'm almost to the ground. O yes, Lord*" . . . But even with all the loss of our parts, we're so blessed; we get to be together, under the same roof. (And I'd sing): "*Sometimes they see me goin' long so. O, yes, Lord*" . . . *You* can seem to be *so* fine; *I* can seem to be so fine; but often nobody really knows what's going on inside us . . . .

They don't have to know, because *Jesus* knows . . . "*Nobody knows the troubles I see . . .*" And that's okay; because, *Jesus, YOU know!* . . . O, yes, Lord! Nobody knows . . . but you, Jesus . . . .

Thanks, Father, that you know what's happening to us. It's not an oversight on your part. You made us. Fearfully, wonderfully, you've made us. Thanks for loving us, Savior. For purchasing us, making us your own property.

Guard over us then, this night, spirit, soul and body.
And wake us up in the joy of your Salvation.

PRAY FOR WISDOM TO UNDERSTAND WHAT'S HAPPENING TO THEM, AND HOW TO RESPOND

Psalm 42:5-6
Soul, why so downcast?

"Why, my soul, are you downcast?
Why so disturbed within me?
Put your hope in God, for I will yet praise him,
my Savior and my God."

The end of that first year was a very hard time. She was crying much of the time. One particular day, she had refused medication all day. She was very aware of where she was, and she spoke it: "I'm afraid . . . What'll I do? . . . What *can* I do?"

I stayed with her the whole day from 11 a.m. on. She was talking clearly: "You're able to go about," she said, "to see people and do things" . . . (inferring, of course: "I can't"). So, I tried to talk to her again, in terms of *seasons* and *trusting God*. And often, I referenced these Psalms 42 and 43 (the two of them together.)

(With Elma) Like a deer, our souls get so thirsty . . . panting . . . frantic . . . out of peace . . . wretched. Tears flow. "Why? Why is this happening to me," we wonder. We're bereft . . . Yet we know where our sufficiency lies. It's in the Creator who formed us and made us for Himself: *"I'll praise him yet. He's my savior; he's my God,"* it says.

But there's a battle for our souls: the enemy hounds us; he taunts us. We look about and we're not sure we like what we see . . . Have we truly been forgotten?. . . Are we alone?. . . And we wonder: "Where are you, God? Have you really abandoned me?"

The Psalmist himself though has been through horrific things; and he reminds us that we can cry out—as we do here in this place, *"God, send us your light . . . We need some light for all this. We need your truth . . . Guide us again into your Presence. We believe we'll be able to praise you yet."*

But I'm not sure it did much good . . . I change the subject and read her some of the James Herriot stories. Three of them. And I'm so relieved that by the end of the evening, at bedtime, she is cheerful, cooperative—she accepts her meds —and she is peaceful. It's a good end of the day.

Father, guard over the spirit of her soul so that she is not attacked by insinuations of "being abandoned and alone." YOU handle that dark enemy for us: "YAH rebukes you, enemy!"[11]

Thank you that your Presence is the safest place for our abiding. Thank you for taking us under the wings of your Tent.

Thank you for the day with Elma. Guard over her heart and mind this entire night. And wake her up in the joy of your Salvation.

---

[11] Zechariah 3:2 along with Jude 8-9 gives that authority over to *YAH* Himself.

THERE IS MORE AT STAKE IN OUR AGING THAN THE PHYSICAL

THERE IS A REAL ENEMY OF OUR SOULS

Psalm 42:3, 4...8...11
My tears . . . my food

"My tears have been my food day and night,
while people say to me all day long,
'Where is your God?'....
I used to go to the house of God
under the protection of the Mighty One
with shouts of joy and praise
among the festive throng....
By day the LORD directs his love,
at night his song is with me—
a prayer to the God of my life."

The crying. Nurses would tell me she's cried while I was gone. By that spring, she was in a kind of sling, within the wheelchair, so as to be easily moved from chair to bed, and bed to chair. But she was no longer propelling the chair manually, and somewhere in the transitions she lost the ability to use her hands at all. No ability to feed herself, or to write, or hold a book—even to scratch her nose.

Jumbled by the dementia, organization of thought was now making speech difficult. And so, on one of those afternoons when I'd come to see her after her nap, as she began to cry, she stammered along with the crying—and finally managed, " . . . I CAN'T . . . GET IT . . . OUT!"

Then—and at other times into that second year when I was with her and she'd start crying—I began to echo back to her her feelings of helplessness. "I know . . . It's so hard . . . the limitations . . . the loss . . . the indignities."

That, and my own crying with her, helped—just to know that I knew, and that she didn't have to tell me.

Psalm 42—and all the other psalms—had been set to music by the Church of Scotland so that they were able *to sing* all of the Psalms. Elma knew this Psalm 42 by heart, and I could talk to her about the words.

(With Elma.) Yes, remember when we used to "go with the multitudes" on Iona, [12] and how, in Detroit and Evansville, we got to be part of the enormous crowds who loved and celebrated God's saving-love. Those were great times. High times. We've had a lot of those, including when you were front-and-center. But now, so quiet, the void . . . after all that storm of activity. And the psalm keeps reminding: *"Put your hope in God."* And over and over: "I'm going to be able yet to praise Him, because He's my Saving God."

But like us, the psalmist is up and down, feeling like a person drowning: ". . . *all your waves and breakers have swept over me.*" And the enemy taunts and says: "O, yeah, *where is your god?*" At the same time, behind the scenes, God is appointing His forces— *"By day, he directs his saving love"*—to break through and reach us. Always His saving-love comes through to help us. And then at night when things can seem so desolate—O yes: the songs. *"His SONG is with us . . . A prayer to the God of my life."* O, how our God exults in *music*— Himself singing to us. He *surrounds* us with "songs of rescue" (Psalm 32:8). He knows. He sees. He is our Saving God, and He comes to help. To save.

(As I sing the evening song . . .) Surround us with your songs, Father. In this room, God. And guard over her heart and mind this night. Give her sweet dreams, and wake her up in the joy of our salvation. (Head-hug. Kiss.)

DO YOUR BEST TO LET THEM KNOW YOU KNOW THE FRUSTRATION, THE LIMITATIONS, THE HELPLESSNESS

---

[12] The ancient Isle of Iona—burial place of Macbeth and other Scottish kings—was location of a retreat center that she'd often been to, and I with her eventually.

Psalm 62: 5-6....8
Pour out your hearts to him

"Yes, my soul, find rest in God;
my hope comes from him.
Truly he is my rock and my salvation;
he is my fortress, I will not be shaken . . .
Trust in him at all times, you people;
pour out your hearts to him,
For God is our refuge."

Elma was sleeping much of the time; and when awake she was eating less and less. Speech was becoming more and more difficult for her. She often was attempting to tell us things, but most of the time I couldn't understand what she was saying. (In my notebook, I recorded the attempts as "ttt"—"trying to talk.") If an aide was present, I'd sometimes ask if she'd understood Elma; and it was usually No.

So, it wasn't just my own hearing—though hearing was an issue. And because I wanted so badly to understand (especially if she was trying to communicate something important to me), I finally cried out to God, "*Father, please—any and every time Elma is saying something* important, *something* essential—*please help me to hear.*" A very important prayer, as it turns out . . . .

(Talking now, with Elma) Old age comes along so sneakily, so unwelcome. But it is not a *forever* season. And with old age's insistent signs comes the nudging, a reminder: that this life here is not "forever," but that there's *more* we're preparing for.

And you know as well, though, that in the meantime, I want so badly to hear you, and *to understand* when you're talking to me . . . But it's such a stretch for me! . . . You know that, don't you? So, with this psalm as reminder, I'm determined *to rest*—and *not stress*—when I'm trying to hear you.

"Find rest, o my soul," it says—namely, *trust.* So, I'm asking, and determined, that I'll be able to *hear* and *understand* whenever you have important things to tell me. "At all times," it says. So, here's an important time again for trusting God for His provision . . .

I had only memorized Psalm 62 through verse 8. So, as I'd often read it that far with Elma, it was a surprise for me when at that point in the psalm she herself finished the verse: *"Trust in him at all times, O people; pour out your hearts to him, for God is our refuge."*

> *Holy One of Israel, you still are full of wonder! Thank you for the gift of this marvelous woman. Son of the Father, nothing shakes you, so we'll also not be shaken. Our strength and our honor depend on you. You, God, are our mighty Rock and our Refuge*

IT'S SO IMPORTANT FOR THEM TO BE ABLE TO COMMUNICATE TO YOU

Psalm 63:1-4, 6-8
You grasp me securely

> *"You, God, are my God, earnestly I seek you;*
> *I thirst for you, my whole being longs for you,*
> *in a dry and parched land*
> *where there is no water.*
> *I have seen you in the sanctuary*
> *And beheld your power and your glory.*
> *Because your love is better than life, my lips will glorify you.*
> *I will praise you as long as I live,*
> *and in your name*
> *I will lift up my hands…*
> *On my bed I remember you; I think of you*
> *through the watches of the night….*
> *Your right hand upholds me."*

She'd lost so many abilities; then, alas, her bathroom independence. I was upset when I found out they'd classified her as "incontinent"—it had gotten increasingly difficult to walk her the few steps from wheelchair to commode, and back—then to see her transferred from chair to bed in this gigantic sling-on-a-derrick and to see that she had to be changed.

Also then at table, to see that her hands could no longer hold a fork and she had to be fed by a CNA or myself. At supper I'd sometimes try to work with her thumb-to-finger exercises; and she was obviously pleased at the effort.

Of course, walking was long since gone. And then, *talk*. She was rightly discouraged by all the losses. Still I read with her the strong scriptures; this one having become by now a standard song.

(As we talk together) It says we have *seen Him in the sanctuary . . . beheld His power and glory . . .* (with sounds of affirmation from Elma). The psalmist jumps up and down to declare that God's "*costly, saving love is better than life itself!*" Better than *life*? . . . Is that so? . . . Life is wonderful, but so tentative, so fragile—and at this point, less than fun. But God's saving love? Over and over, this and other psalms attest, "*His saving love is FOREVER.*" It's the thing that lasts . . . . . so that it's the thing to be *sung* about! To raise our hands in His Name. To jump and shout about. (I'll have to do so for both of us . . .)

With the coming of night—and that room becoming so empty and dark as I leave—I read and say with her, "*On my bed I remember you. I think of you through the watches of the night. For because you've helped me, I sing! . . . In the shadow of your wings, I sing.*"

And then because of the assurance which she needed—and which I could never give—at times I'd tell her again Jesus' story of The Midnight Visitor, and of our next-door, Neighbor/ Covenant-God, who is pledged to us—always, no matter how untimely, no matter the expense—to get up and bring us all and everything never available in our own cupboards, but so fully supplied in His: safety, security, protection. All.

And then we'd pray—and this, over and over through the months— "*My soul clings to you. And with your right hand, you hold and grasp ME securely*" (verse 8 as I applied it with her).

O God our God, darkness is not dark to you. The dark shines like the day to you. Thanks for knowing us so, loving us, abiding with us, never abandoning us, but holding us securely, entirely yours, forever in your Presence.

REMIND AND RE-INSTRUCT ON THE MATTERS OF GOD'S FAITHFUL GRASP OF US, NO MATTER OUR CIRCUMSTANCES

Psalm 62:1-3
Find rest, my soul

"Truly my soul finds rest in God; my salvation comes from him;
He alone is my rock and my salvation . . .
How long will you assault me? . . .
this leaning wall, this tottering fence?"

I still start my day, early morning every day, asking to be able "to love her well, and to love her wisely." But I'm tired.

How do I rest? I feel like I'm on a marathon . . . swamped . . . go, go, go . . . And then I read, *"My soul finds rest in God alone."* But where's the rest? —the grace?

Help me. I know I'm going at this wrong, Jesus. *"My rest is in you, God alone,"* it says. And you are rest for the over-burdened. Being yoked to you is easy and gives rest for the soul (it says here).

But the Enemy taunts; he assaults. I keep feeling that Elma's total welfare is my responsibility. I look at every sign of need or difficulty in her as my obligation—mine to fix. Though I've been warned about that, my flesh keeps assigning me jobs in my weekly planner; and I'm having a hard time letting go.

Hebrews 3-4 says: Rest comes with hearing your voice, and in not hardening my heart . . . Is my heart hardened? . . . Whatever it is, help! I badly need your help.

Help me, Father. I'm foolish. Forgive me for low trust. For lack of
trust. For trust barely flickering. Help me to quiet flesh's slave-driving
voice. Help me to have your wisdom in this thing of loving Elma.

*But I thank you for the rare privilege of getting to love her. It's
so wonderful, Savior; I'm so grateful, and I love you.*

YOU CAN GET TOO ISOLATED, TOO PROUD, TOO SELF-SUFFICIENT

THERE IS A HARD BALANCE TO FIND . . . BETWEEN TRYING TO DO EVERYTHING AND NOT DOING ENOUGH

Psalm 31:9-10...14-15...21
Intervening love

*"Me merciful to me, LORD, for I am in distress;
My eyes grow weak with sorrow, my soul and body with grief.
My life is consumed by anguish and my years by groaning;
my strength fails because of my affliction,
and my bones grow weak....
But I trust in you, LORD; I say, 'You are my God'.
My times are in your hands...
Praise be to the LORD, for he showed me the wonders
of his love when I was in a city under siege."*

We're in a tight little double room nearest the nurse's station where she'd now been moved, and where there's an unhappy roommate who keeps yelling at us . . . (Poor dear!)

(Reading this with Elma): Oh, yes, Lord: "*under siege!*" Our times are in your hands, including those times when we have been so secure, so confident; and you have enabled us to do so many things in our lives.

Elma, like the time when you, as part of your probation officer training, had to supervise and corral a bunch of young girls, wards of the court, in the berry-picking endeavor. They'd seen these young boys around and were forever trying to sneak away for a tryst . . . one even trying to escape across a railway bridge, and you had to give chase . . . Or the times you'd been in charge of a regional mothers' conference—organizing the seventy-some workshops—and took our kids out of school to help you collate materials. Ages 5 to 10 they were, but you had them practiced and adept at circling the table to collate the hundreds of packets for the registrants. What a circus!—but *an organized circus,* you'd be sure . . .

So many things we've each gotten to do . . . ! Wonderful times!

But then there are the times, like now, when we don't like how this part of our story is turning out. The Psalmist sounds like he knows what it's like to get *old!* . . . weak . . . groaning . . . sorrow . . . anguish. Well, we're "in a besieged city"—maybe besieged not with bullets—but with the multiple afflictions *of age!* Needing help for nearly everything . . .

So, it's so good to be able to call upon a God who *intervenes* with His saving love*!* who has totally come into our place, experienced/ suffered everything we will ever know (now, in this and in any human circumstance)—in His being buffeted and abused as Victim. Even for Him to know the helplessness of this season that we're in, but *breaking the power of our enemy* for us[13]—in this, as in any other circumstance we've been in.

So, thank you for giving us the experiences of our life, and for proving yourself Savior in every circumstance along the way.

Thank you that you, Jesus, have become flesh of our flesh, bone of our bone, in order to destroy the power of the enemy over us, to break us free and prepare us for your Big Plans and promises. (Hebrews 2:14)

REMIND THEM OF THEIR STORIES--- SOME OF THE THINGS THEY'VE BEEN BLESSED TO GET TO DO

---

[13] Hebrews 2:14-15.

Psalm 31:7-8
You knew the anguish

"I will be glad and rejoice in your love,
for you saw my affliction
and knew the anguish of my soul.
You have not given me over into the hands of the enemy
but have set my feet in a spacious place."

After lunch, now with too little time to get to our apartment before her nap, we frequently have to find sanctuary someplace away from her room. So, seasonally, when the patio isn't an option, we check out the little anteroom at the end of the corridor, or the little adjunct Dining Room. But the bedtimes in her room are so precious.

(Our talk time together) Oh, the *wonder of our God!* He doesn't miss anything. He absolutely knows what's happening to us. And He's got it covered. He's got us in hand. He's doing a thing in us, getting us ready for that marvelous amazing time when we transition out of here. All the things that could have thrown our lives . . . the way the enemy had conspired to destroy me, to bring you down . . . Our God has got between us and the enemy; He's interfered, intervened for us! He "saw my affliction"; He knew the anguish of your soul; but He didn't just leave us to the wiles of the enemy.

He took hold of us and planted our feet in a *spacious place.* All the stuff we've been through in our lives, Elma. The stuff that could have wrecked us and destroyed us; but His blood-sworn, saving, committed love didn't let go of us.

And even in these times, in this season so strange to us—this old age season when my legs don't work right, and my hearing's going, and a bunch of other parts aren't so sure—we're in a BROAD PLACE. We've got our little three-room apartment; we've got our meals taken care of, and nursing care. And most of all, we get to be in this place where we're together. We're with each other *almost all the day* . . . And we love each other, and get to spend these precious evening times together. O, Elma, *we're blessed.*

And Father, you're so good. Guard over my Elma this night, spirit, soul, and body. And wake her up in the joy of your salvation.

REAFFIRM THE GOOD THINGS
ABOUT THEIR SITUATION

Finding Secure Currents In Christ Jesus

Psalm 32:7
You are my Hiding Place

"You are my hiding place;
you will protect me from trouble[14]
and surround me with
songs of deliverance."

Her room is getting impossible to talk in during the day. The roommate is mellowing, but she now wants to chime into our talk (her hearing is great)—and she's *loud!* Bedtimes, though, she's usually asleep by the time of our night talks, so that's a relief.

(Talking with Elma, one of our nighttime moments) I'm so glad to have memorized these various psalms in the last ten years. And this is one I've loved.

But it's so much stronger in the immediate/present tense. The Hebrew future/present verb implies both "now" and "coming to be." So, rather than read it: "You *will* protect me from trouble"—anticipating help in whatever future time —I read this one and many others with an immediacy, a now/present help. "You ARE my hiding place."

He is our hiding place. Even now, and constantly, He has been protecting us from trouble. And, o yes—He surrounds us with SONGS. We're surrounded by His singing! He loves to sing to us. And they are songs that tell of His rescue, His saving, His determining at every point to break in and bring us out.

---

[14] As in previous note, the Hebrew present/future verb offers the option of either tense. The present in this case is again much stronger and more immediate: "...*you do protect me from trouble.*"

I love the knowledge that our God is the God *who made music*, who *talks* through music, who *hears* through music, who hears the cries of the heart that only music can communicate, who honors the love songs of psalmists everywhere, and of love songs that we sing to each other. And I believe He is unmoved, but forbearing, with mediocre melody and hates wretched/debauched lyrics and its accompanying din.

Music is of the Spirit. It rises with us in the mornings, and it carries in our heads all the day. With song He stirred my dad to reach beyond himself when the heart attack kept him from sleep night after night and led him to pray the prayers that saved my life. With song, our God interrupts me—unsuspected, but there it is: the same faith-song to encourage or redirect me. Over and over, He brings it to my mind:

"Jesus, Jesus, how I trust him! How I've proved him o'er and
o'er. Jesus, Jesus, precious Jesus! Oh, for grace to trust him more.
I'm so glad I learned to trust him: precious Jesus, Savior, Friend;
*And I know **that** he is with me; he is with me to the end."*[15]

USE MUSIC. USE PSALMS.

Psalm 23: 5-6
A table set before me

"You prepare a table before me in the presence of my enemies.
You anoint my head with oil; my cup overflows.
Surely your goodness and love will follow me
all the days of my life,
and I will dwell in the house of the LORD forever."

Standard fare for us were the stories of the young Scottish veterinarian, James Herriot. His book, *All Creatures Great and Small*, went with us in my "pickup-truck" (my four-wheeled walker with its storage basket under

---

[15] "'Tis so sweet to trust in Jesus," Celebration Hymnal, #581.

the raised seat). We read his tales everywhere we parked—more and more occasions on the patio as the season warmed up. Many of his tales about sheep—and lambing, with the vet's arm ever-immersed to the shoulder in a ewe . . .

But I was writing at the time about near-eastern hospitality; so that too became a subject of our reflections. And the beleaguered sheep of the Twenty-Third Psalm . . . transmutes to find himself "guest" in the tent of the Shepherd.

(Our talk time together, first on the patio; then at her bed): Jesus lets us know we've become more than sheep to him when he talks about finding us and taking us into his own tent. There may be enemies all around; but it doesn't matter. For in his tent we're totally safe, vouched for by commitment of his very life. And we're able to rest secure as he caters to us with the very best he has: we're the valued, honored guest. Nothing spared to us. Our cups are filled with the best wine. Our heads anointed with fine oil . . .

When our little brief tryst is over, he sends us on to our final destination, the House of his Father, where we're to live as sons and daughters of His Forever Family. And, in the meantime, he blesses us by securing our safety—with the same "goodness and blood-sworn, saving love"[16] pledged to follow and secure us—for all of whatever days remain.

Elma, we are so covenantally-*secured* by this Shepherd-Savior God of ours.

Secure her this night, O Lord our God. You are our Hiding Place. You protect us from trouble and surround us with songs of deliverance. Thanks for this day in your presence, and wake us up in the Joy of your Salvation.

LET THEM BE SURROUNDED WITH SECURING WORDS, GOD'S WORDS, YOUR WORDS

---

[16] The essential socio-cultural aspect of the Hebrew word, *khesed* (so much bigger than "mercy")—as the hospitality in the Near East, where a host-family guarantees the safety and provision of its guests at the cost of their own lives—was opened up by Nelson Glueck's pivotal research (1927) and elaborated by a score of eminent Biblical scholars. However, this essential scholarship was not translated into English until (1967), three years after the Brown, Driver, Briggs commentary had anchored *khesed* as mere "mercy" (1964).

Psalm 63:6, 8
On my bed I remember you

*"On my bed I remember you; I think of you through
the watches of the night…..I cling to you;
your right hand upholds me."*

I read this one often with her—one of our favorites, telling of God's secure hold of us. But I also try to imagine how she's seeing things, how all this must seem to her:

The wheelchair, now so confining. It circumscribes my life, seeking to define my limits. It encases my arms, cradles my head, elevates my feet . . . I can't turn or shift my body, but I can lift my arms and turn my head.

Each day I get to trundle down the hall to the two little rooms he calls "Our Apartment." There I'm tilted up, or I'm tilted down—to get pressure off my bum—all depending on whether I need to sleep more or not. If I'm awake, often we have music, sometimes the sounds of home with Celtic bagpipes wailing, or of bluegrass, but mostly philharmonic . . . Occasionally he'll have the TV on for me. Sometimes we watch a documentary together.

Usually he's on the computer: sometimes he reads me what he's been writing. I so hunger for the stimulation of thought and speech . . . Evenings for a while we read together a history of the Scots Irish.

When he has company, and if I'm awake—I love the times—I get to hear the discussion. I try to enter in sometimes, but I'm having such a hard time now getting my thoughts out of my mouth.

We're together almost constantly. Most of the morning, in the apartment. Then again after lunch. Then evenings and bedtime. Sometimes, when his feet will take him, we have a little walk outside, or to the parlor to enjoy the sunshine coming in the east windows and see the beauty of the circle of lilies, aflame in colors.

Sometimes—on many bonny days—I'm taken out through the patio door, and we sit out surrounded by the sky, the over-looming trees, and watch the skidding clouds or hear a story of the Scottish vet in the Yorkshire country . . .

There is supper together, maybe while watching episodes of "Little House on the Prairie." Then, bed.

O yes, bed. The bed is *so good* sometimes. And there, the talk, the scriptures, the songs, the prayer. And there the reminder of your strong, securing Presence . . . .

I thank you for those who care for my bodily needs. Certain caregivers are
so faithful to see me lifted gently, and lovingly washed and bedded down.
Some still need to learn to honor and care for someone such as I now am.
See mercifully to those ones, LORD.
But thanks for my bed, the darkened room, and the gift of sleep

HELP THEM TO HAVE SOME CONTENT TO THEIR LIVES

TRY TO IMAGINE HOW IT MIGHT ALL SEEM TO THEM

Psalm 18:19
You delighted in me

"He rescued me because he delighted in me."

What a struggle it was . . .

Oh, but what a joy that it's done.

She had given me hints of an anxiety, a grief . . . I didn't know if I'd heard right. (It was always a constant effort, with my hearing loss, to wonder at what Elma was saying). That second summer, just after having come on hospice, I heard *those doubts.* I didn't know what to think. Along with the tears, she was trying to tell me something, and I didn't know how to hear it right. Some indications of "not believing" . . .

Then, a month or so later, she'd gotten real sick. Hospice was saying the time is near. The bulk of her medications were curtailed. "No point . . . the antibiotics won't help anymore." But then I heard those fragmented comments from her—and crying. I had said some things of faith to her, and she countered with: "No," and, "I don't believe." She was sobbing. I tried to make sure if I was understanding: "Are you saying . . . " (I tried to ask). But she repeated clearly: "Half yes, and half no." I was tempted to argue, but there were more tears, and no consolation.

So, all through the rest of that day as I reflected—and as I searched God in prayer that night and next morning—I recalled a series of hurtful things in her life. Resolve, toughness on her part. Profound biblical knowledge. But I could recall no instance—in order to counter those things on her behalf—of her *personally embracing* the work accomplished for us by the Lord Jesus on the Cross.

So, the next afternoon with her, when she woke up sobbing again, I took her to that same small dining room where we could have some privacy. I explained what I'd been recalling of things she'd told me over the years, and that I'd never heard on any occasion of her taking to herself those crucial things done on our behalf by Christ. I urged her to say her own "Yes" to all that, and she balked. Then she tried but couldn't say it. She just couldn't get the word out. I kept urging her, and finally, with great struggle . . . and with a great sigh . . . she managed finally to get out a "YES" to it all . . . !

From that day on, and in the months following—for she didn't die as they thought—all the staff kept exclaiming: "Look at her: Elma's so happy!" "She's beaming." "She's so beautiful!" And, right up to the last month, I would hear from complete strangers in the dining room: "Oh. She's so beautiful." (It was almost embarrassing.) Don't say it. I don't want her to have to struggle now with *being vain* as well . . .

> *Lord, you're good and your Saving Initiative is forever—*
> *you don't quit on us just because we're old and left-behind.*
> *Thanks for rescuing us. Thanks for delighting in us.*
>
> *I praise you for giving Elma words still to communicate her*
> *heart, and for giving me ears to hear your Spirit. And I bless*
> *you for the beauty of how you work in my beloved's life.*

PRAY TO UNDERSTAND WHATEVER YOU NEED TO UNDERSTAND

Psalm 118: 14-18
Shouts of joy and victory

"Shouts of joy and victory resound in the tents of the righteous:
'The LORD's right hand has done mighty things!
The LORD's right hand is lifted high;
The LORD's right hand has done mighty things!'
I will not die but live,
and will proclaim what the LORD has done.
The LORD has chastened me severely,
but he has not given me over to death."

(With you, LORD, and Elma—both) It is such a relief to know victory won. It's not just once in our lives, but many times. Each time, to realize that we've been in a desperate spot, and that the LORD—way beyond anything we pulled off—has intervened, shown Himself the helper, *the One who did it!*

Then we can say, over and over—yes, *we can SING it*—"YAH, *you are my Strength and my Song."* And we can recognize it, that this was no coincidence. You not only brought me through, but more than that, "Jesus, you've shown yourself again my Rescuer. My Champion. The One who is My Salvation."

So, how do we want to live? . . . We want to live letting it be known *what you do, and Who you are!* The marvels of it: we didn't die (not yet I know). But we also know that this One who is Savior is also the One who specifically and pointedly has taken us through difficult stuff *in order to train us*—yes, to "chasten" us.

Elma, we've been *brought through!* I know we're not done yet but we're his! We're in his hands! And by the sworn covenant-in-his-blood, he's committed to carrying us through.

I will sing to the God of Creation.
I will sing to the Lord of Life, Everlasting Life, Everlasting Life.
I will rise so early in the morning,
Rise to sing my Savior's praises.

Rise, with joy in my heart, to greet the LORD who gives
me life, Everlasting Life, Everlasting Life . . . .[17]

CELEBRATE THE WONDERS: EACH AND EVERY TIME GOD BRINGS US THROUGH SOMETHING

Psalm 30: 1...4, 5...11
From wailing to dancing

"...you lifted me out of the depths
and did not let my enemies gloat over me...
Sing the praises of the LORD, you his faithful people...
weeping may stay for the night,
but rejoicing comes in the morning...
You turned my wailing into dancing."

Occasionally when our daughter Jennifer visited—especially once the mood had changed—she would sometimes crawl in bed with Elma (her "Mum"), just often for a cuddle with her, but then also for the laughs between them. The two of them would look at each other and beam foolishly, crazily.

I tried it twice: crawling in with Elma; but then I had a hard time crawling back out again . . .

(With Elma) This psalm is almost autobiographical, as you know. I could have been destroyed by the things happening to me when I was young, but I wasn't. All God's purposes for me could have been undermined by the ugliness imprinted on my soul. But they weren't. And you, too, the things you've had to struggle with. But He "lifted me out of the depths," it says . . . and didn't let my enemies *gloat* over me. (O, yes!) "*LORD, my God, I called to you for help and you healed me.*" (v. 2)

So, we've got good reason to *sing!*

I like it that we're called to sing! And, oh, it says: "*You turned my wailing into dancing. You removed my sackcloth and clothed me with joy!*" (v.

---

[17] Public domain. Author/composer unknown.

11) Elma, we still get to *dance!* Dance? —o yes, often we still danced—the jitterbug movements, *seated* now because of my legs. Comic probably, if you're watching. But fun. Laughs. (That old feeling.)

> *I exalt you, our God, for bringing us up "out of the pit." I'm so glad. Let my heart sing to you, LORD, and not be silent.*
>
> *O LORD my God, I will give you thanks as long as I have life and breath. And then, in the next breath, praise you forever!*

TELL THE STORIES OF GOD'S FAITHFULNESS. ENJOY. LAUGH.

2 Corinthian 4:7...10
These earthen vessels

> *"But we have this treasure in jars of clay....*
> *We always carry around in our body the death of Jesus,*
> *so that the life of Jesus may also*
> *be revealed in our body."*

At every chance possible, we're on The Patio. It's our special place. Usually it's just us; but then from time-to-time other family members of patients find and relish the space, and we get to talk to and know them. But, also in her dining room, we get into conversations with family members, as well as CNAs as they're feeding other patients at our table.

I never wanted Elma to feel abandoned. And that can put a terrible pressure on you if persons are the demanding type. For, in their new situation of helplessness or confusion, we need to understand: Life can be painfully lonely. And terribly boring. Or scary.

I never felt that kind of pressure from Elma. But there were occasional little bouts of jealousy—and no wonder! You've lost everything else about yourself; and you don't want to lose the major people of your life . . . ! Once in that first traumatic ten days, when our daughter had come down just for "a day of loving Elma," Elma became miffed at seeing her chat to the other persons around us and closed her face to her, to our daughter's great hurt.

At other times over the next waning months (with Elma by then greatly restricted in speech), if she saw me speaking too much to the other families, or to an aide, she would pull away and close her face to me.

Privately, I chided her about the jealousy. I told her then (and on another occasion about a different matter) that that was a selfish thing on her part—"It's important for me to be able to talk with people who are around us . . ." And "selfishness on our parts needs to die . . ." (It may surprise, but she was able to take that in and accept it.)

On occasions of talk and scripture time, I read with her from this powerfully beautiful passage about "the death of Jesus" happening in our own bodies.

(As we reflect about it together) It is a mysterious thing observed by the apostle here: the "death of Jesus" at work in the bodies of believers. It's another stab at describing the ultimate work which the Creator/Savior God is doing in us . . . whether He gets our cooperation or not—that "conforming work" talked about in Romans 8:29—with the end-product in mind of making us *recognizable* "little brothers and sisters" in the family of the First-Born, our Lord Jesus.

It's the dying-and-rising with Jesus, which Jesus so pointedly called for—and which we so happily attempt to dodge in our Gospel reading and devotionals: that there's stuff in every one of us (beloved of God), that *has to die!* . . . in order that His Life may then *also "be revealed in our body."*

In so many ways, all our life—in losses and disappointments and frustrations—we're constantly "*being given over to death for Jesus' sake, so that his life may be revealed in our mortal body.*" (vs.11) Little matters of ugliness and The Rebellion that have to die . . .

> *Father, how you love us! So precious to you we are, that*
> *you've put your treasure in these earthen vessels.*

I thank you for the beauty of your presence in my spectacular lady.
I'm so proud of this woman, and so grateful, loving Savior, for your
patience with us and the beautiful things you're doing in us.

SOME MAY TRY TO DOMINATE YOU AND DEMAND UNREALISTIC THINGS OF YOU.

Psalm 118
His saving love is forever

"Give thanks to the LORD, for he is good!
his love endures forever.
Let Israel say…let the House of Aaron say…
let those who fear the LORD say :
'HIS LOVE ENDURES FOREVER!'" (vv. 1-4)

(With Elma) Not just for some time. Not just for later. The saving love of the LORD is *always.* "Forever" is how long He has determined to save us, to call us, to know us. It's "the mystery" kept secret for ages (Romans 16:25-26), the costly plan now made known in the coming and intervening of His Son.

It's *always,* we can now say: in whatever imaginable circumstance, He is *always intent and committed* to save us. To intervene. Israel needed to know it. The priestly House of Aaron needed to know it. And now those of us, who've come to fear and love God through His Son, need also to know it.

He hasn't forgotten us. In our dotage He hasn't forgotten us. Even here in this situation, in this season, He's still got us in His hand. As we look around and see some who *seem "abandoned"* (some souls in nursing, for instance)— even in them He is working, accomplishing things in their last days.

For some, He is still making openings for them to know Him— "pen-ultimately," as you'd love to say.[18] With others, as with you and me, He is secretly, quietly *"putting to death"* some of our unworthy things—

---

[18]   Elma liked *words!* And she enjoyed the word "penultimate" —the next to the last thing *just before the very last "ultimate" thing!*

some of the pride, the stupid selfishness, etc.—which can't come along with us if we're going *IN*.

But we can rejoice to know that His saving love is forever. We're the objects of it. We're in its embrace.

Praise the LORD. He is with me; I'm not afraid: what can anyone do to me. He is with me. He is my helper; I will look with triumph on my enemies . . . Shouts of joy and victory. the LORD has done mighty things.

I will not die but proclaim what He has done. He has chastened me severely, but not given me over to death. HalleluYah!

HELP THEM ARTICULATE PRAISE FOR GOD'S CONSTANT, SAVING HELP

Psalm 31: 2-4
For sake of your Name

"...be my rock of refuge,
a strong fortress to save me.
Since you are my rock and my fortress,
for the sake of your name lead and guide me.
Free me from the trap that is set for me,
for you are my refuge."

Stories continued important. More and more I began to recite some of our adventures—like in our thorny move to southern Indiana.

(Recalling the story with Elma) You remember the difficulty in leaving Detroit . . . We'd gotten this call for me to come as director of a conference center in the little utopian town. We'd been invited once, twice, three times—even the chance to spend a summer there and check it out. But each time—the red flags were profuse! It shrieked with warnings: *Don't come!* But the summer had tantalizingly opened up friend-ships there—including with two young Christian theatre people, as you know—friendships significant enough that we're now the godparents for their children.

The warnings were so ominous. But I needed to make a decision. My school teaching term was about to start again; and—the real motivator—your Dad was about to come from Scotland for another three-month stay. He'd already had questions about my "checkered career" (leading his daughter into inner-city America, among other eyebrow-raising things). So, I dreaded having him again ask about my current employment . . .

I'd been praying desperately for direction. Finally, you remember, I did that questionable thing: I'd heard about "Gideon fleeces." (Whatever possessed me to do such a thing? . . .) Anyway, I chanced offering up a Gideon fleece—a truly unlikely thing that went like this: *"God, if you want us to go to _____, let me hear from two people there by tomorrow night midnight."* (Thinking "phone calls.")

The next day there were two letters in the mail from persons in that town . . . Interesting, I thought; but that doesn't count: those letters were already in the mail before I posed my offer to God . . . Then it hit me, the staggering thought: God had already prompted those two persons, independently, each to write and mail me letters—*before His prompting me then* to pose such an inane request to Him . . . !

The reassurance—of the rightness of that move to that town as you know—proved essential for us in the months to come. We needed that certainty of God's leading. For in our going there, we had to face and deal with so many things, *so over our heads*—spiritual giants!—which, without the clear leading of the Lord, would otherwise have had us scurrying back to Detroit, bewildered and whipped.

Instead, we avoided traps. We were sorely tested and tried there— but *majorly schooled,* expanded and blest.

God is our Rock. He does lead; and it's for His own Name's sake that He does so. It's important that we ask for things that will suit His Name, for His Name is always at stake in how and where He leads His people . . .

Thank you, our Father. Praise you, Jesus our hiding place.
Oh, how you've carried us, way beyond our knowing. For your
Name's sake, help us even now to trust you in these days.

Guard over Elma this night. Wake her in the
joy of our salvation. (Hugs, kisses.)

RECALL STORIES OF GOD IN HIS FAITHFULNESS

Colossians 3:3-4
Hidden in Christ Jesus

"For you died, and your life
is now hidden with Christ in God.
When Christ, who is your life, appears,
then you also will appear with him in glory.

Elma thrived on ideas. She and I loved to talk. We talked about everything, from our first friendship on. Even in dementia, she relished ideas as she watched documentaries with me—and responded with evidence that she understood. As I read the Scots Irish history to her (*Born Fighting*), or portions of my manuscript, her face would brighten. (But then, of course, sometimes I get carried away, as—on one night, at bedtime—when she was tired; and she said, "Enough talk.")

So, I was able to talk scriptures with her to reinforce her confidence. And she understood what we read—as with this scripture from Colossians . . . .

(Our talk time together) Jesus has acquired for us *an intimacy!* A closeness. Tight! We don't want to miss out on it, it's so expensively acquired. Acquired by his *blood*. It is a sealed, covenanted closeness. The way Jesus describes it is beyond picturing or diagram. For he says it's the same as the intimacy *he has* with his Father. So close that he *does—only what he sees his Father doing. And says—only what he hears his Father saying!* (John 5:19, 8:28)

Then he drops on believers the astonishing promise that —when he'd have come through the Crucifixion and had been raised to life again by the Father—"*On that day you will realize that I am in my Father*, and *you are in me* and I am *in you.*" (John 14:20) Such a closeness! It's a gift. We can rest in it. Live in it. Walk in it.

But it's "hidden." Our LIFE—the beauty of all of our life as redeemed in our Lord Jesus Christ—*is hidden* to us. And its beauty will be seen only when Christ Jesus *is unwrapped to be seen*, and when *we're unwrapped*, in him and with him.

> *O, yes, "Let the beauty of Jesus be seen in me. All his wonderful passion and purity. O, You Spirit Divine, all our natures refine, 'til the beauty of Jesus be seen in me."[19]*

IF TALKING TOGETHER HAS BEEN IMPORTANT FOR YOU, THEN IT CAN CONTINUE TO BE.

Psalm 34:4-6....9
This poor man called

> *"I sought the LORD, and he answered me;*
> *he delivered me from all my fears.*
> *Those who look to him are radiant;*
> *their faces are never covered with shame.*
> *This poor man called, and the LORD heard him;*
> *he saved him out of all his troubles....*
> *Fear the LORD, you his holy people,*
> *for those who fear him lack nothing."*

I realize I'm tired.

When's the last time I had a vacation? A weekend off? How long will I be able to keep this up? (But I don't say any of this to anyone.)

Those good times in the apartment continued, with little chats in between naps. As for the naps, they were not only for her, but for me. We'd frequently nap together, she in her wheelchair, tilted down and parked parallel to my single-bed (head-to-foot, foot-to-head) so I could observe her as I awoke. She might even be wakeful as I slept; but either way there was a contentment in being nearby.

The afternoons were changing, however. The unit nurse said that Elma

---

[19] By Albert Orsbom/Tom M. Jones. Public domain.

needed rest in her bed after lunch, and relief from the wheelchair. So that time together was shortened. But I'd still come see her immediately after lunch and have that bit of time together.

I continued reading scripture to her at bedtime, her face always responsive to the words.

(With Elma) This one is for both of us. You're tired, and I am too. We're both wondering, "How long is this going to go on?" But then here's this psalm. It begins with the person wanting to *"boast* on the LORD"—as someone who's newly in love with God might do—and inviting others around to join in, however down they are, however assailed or "poorly" they may feel. He tells of how God rescued him out of his own fears. And he points to other amazing people around him whose faces *shine*. (You shine, Elma. And we think of friends of ours who *glow*.) They've learned to fear God, knowing He's *good*.

That the Heavenly Father is *good* is an amazing discovery! Fearing Him now is to trust His wisdom on all matters. To trust His goodness. To trust His ability to take care of things we fear—things like timing . . . and readiness . . . and other things that may be involved. Then He points us away from ourselves: even *"the lions may grow weak and hungry, but those who seek the LORD lack no good thing."* (vs. 10)

We're called like that: to know again that everything is okay, and to know that we're going to have everything we may need the moment we need it—like the little girl whose papa, on their train journeys together, always gave her her token just the moment she needed it for the turn-style . . . .

Jesus, you trusted all fearful things into the hands of your Father.
Help us to do it too when we're afraid. Help us to trust your
Father as you do. Over and over, you've carried us through
in times past. Help us to trust you in this time too.

As the hymn says:[20] *Precious Lord, take my hand....I am tired, I am*
weak, I am worn. Through the storm, through the night, lead me
on to the Light. Take my hand, precious Lord, lead me home.

IT CAN SEEM LIKE A NEVER-ENDING MARATHON

---

[20] Celebration Hymnal, #684.

Psalm 23:5
My cup overflows

"...in the presence of my enemies
....my cup overflows."

She had been moved now to a single room nearest the nurse's station—for closer observation presumably. It was a room with three big windows and a great glimpse of garden just outside the windows—and across from the room where I and other residents had our exercise classes. I pointed to that room across the garden to her one day, saying that that's where we exercise, and she said, "I know." (A surprise to me: that *orientation* and *memory* both were still there for her.)

Also, we were still having our times outdoors at the patio. One evening there on patio, she exulted, "What are we to do with all this beauty . . .!"

She often said, "I love you"; and for times when she didn't have the energy to talk, she created her own "blink" signals: one blink ("yes"); two blinks (kisses); three blinks ("I love you").

And she would be funny! As she was being put to bed one night—in the sling, lifted off her wheelchair by the machine—she remarked to whoever was listening, "....O, the drama of the situation!" And then another time, a morning, as I came to see her at the end of breakfast and called her oatmeal "gruel," she *hooted* with laughter. She loved to tease; and if at times she couldn't do it verbally, she did it facially, with eyes and tilt of head.

Then too, sometimes if the hospice nurse would come around and she wasn't sound asleep, she could have a smart-alec greeting for her, eyes acknowledging her fun. Or as, out on the patio once, when I challenged her with: "I thought you'd have something to say about that," "Not I" was her reply, eyes full of mischief.

All this after her shutting down those many months and being consigned to hospice. Over and over in that last year, Elma would level out, then sink near death, over and over raising question whether she still qualified for hospice . . . .

(Reading this portion of Psalm 23 with Elma): Do you know how blessed we are! No matter what else is happening all around us, under the protective covering of the Good Shepherd—look at us. We get to have all this beauty, and time together—and still to love and enjoy each other.

Our cup runs over, it's so amazing. God is good: we're well taken care of!

DON'T ASSUME THERE'S NOTHING THERE JUST BECAUSE THE PERSON IS IN DEMENTIA.

ENJOY THE FULLNESS OF THE MOMENTS.

Psalm 71:17-18
Do not forsake me…old & gray

"Since my youth, God, you have taught me,
and to this day I declare your marvelous deeds.
Even when I am old and gray, do not forsake me, my God,
till I declare your power to the next generation,
your might to all who are to come."

December of that year I became sick—three years into her final season. Family arranged for me to get some days at our daughter's in Indy, three hours away. The sons would cover me, spend time with Elma. When I told her, trying to explain my need, she cried. She searched my face for reassurance and seemed to understand as I left.

I was gone for five days, enough time to feel somewhat better but eager to come back, worried how she'd be.

She wasn't glad to see me. She wouldn't look at me at first; and when she did, she began crying, and said, "WEEKS!" —eyebrows and voice both raised for emphasis! (I had to laugh even then as I held her, she was so mad.)

Within five days I was as sick as before; so, another trip to Indy followed—this time for *ten days.*

On my coming back, this time Elma would look at and chat to staff members, but not me. It took several days. When again I told her how I'd missed her, there were sobs and then, finally—at bedtime—happy recognition with multiple blinks and the welcome and verbal "I love you."

(With Elma, holding her.) I know it's hard. To be away. To be apart. But you know, don't you, that I had to be away? I couldn't breathe, I couldn't sleep.

Elma, we never know which of us is going to go first. But God is good, and I have to trust Him in that. Meanwhile, we have things to live for, and things to pass on to our children and grandchildren: God's power and might, and what He has done with us. Along with that I have to trust, that if I go first and you're left alone, God *will carry and hold you* . . . I have to believe that also . . . that if you go first, He'll *carry and hold me.*

It's tough. But, if you think about it, that's what we both took on when we made those vows fifty-some years ago. (Some tears, and some holding; and then some acceptance of what I'd said.) But look at us: we're together again; and we love each other so much. And it's *good,* isn't it?

From birth we have relied on you; you brought us forth
from our mothers' wombs. We'll praise you forever. (71:6)
We know you don't cast us away when we're old;
that you don't forsake us when our strength is gone. (71:9)

Guard over our hearts and minds now, as you keep us in Christ Jesus.

AS FOR YOUR OWN HEALTH, NO ASSURANCE THAT YOU WON'T GO FIRST

2 Timothy 1:12-13
The deposit is safe

"I know that safe with him remains,
protected by His power,
what I've committed to His trust
'til the decisive hour. . ."
[Isaac Watts hymn][21]

Six days later she was sick, with high fever—the first of three times she was deathly ill in the next ten months. Hospice advised against the course of antibiotics: it would do no good, they said, for the infection would take over and the end would come rather quickly. But, within a day or more, Elma threw off the infection. Then again, in May, mid-July, and mid-September, the same thing. They began to call her "Miss Bounce," because she bounced back so fast—not only in wellness, but cheerfulness.

(With Elma) The apostle Paul said it first, that he was convinced that God is *able to guard what I have entrusted to him until that day...* (2 Tim. 1:12) And you've sung it most of your life: *I know that safe with him remains, protected by his power: what I've committed to his trust....* Everything about us, everything we've lived for in Christ, everything we've offered to him—family, church, leadership, and however each eventually turns out—all of it is entrusted to Him, to those competent, Crucified and Risen Hands; and it's all held securely there.

He's given us our times. We've had adventurous and marvelous times to get to do things . . . . to take responsibility . . . to create and develop . . . to know . . . to love . . . to invest in friendships—and we are *rich in friendships!* All those things we've done: the conference directing, coaching of teachers and speakers and mothers, the child birthing and nurturing of children, the coping with big things and standing for important things—all of that, we've had our time for doing.

And it's all in Him now . . . It's His . . . And He's good . . . He knows what's good . . . and what He can use . . . and what He can trash. But He holds it all. And He holds us. And that's all that matters from here on out.

---

[21] Third verse of hymn by Isaac Watts, "I'm not ashamed to own my Lord." From Scottish Hymnal, public domain.

We are yours, Lord. And everything we've done is yours. Thanks for those times then, for these times now: the times here sitting out on the patio enjoying the space, the unfettered time, the quiet, your caring and provision.

Thanks for these CNAs who make it seem like it's no trouble to bring our trays out here and cater to us.

Thanks for kind people and faithful friends. Thanks that all is secure in you.

TALK ABOUT THE WORTHY ACTIVITIES WE'VE BEEN IN, AS WELL AS THINGS GOD HAS BROUGHT US THROUGH

Psalm 25:15
Eyes ever on The LORD

"My eyes are ever on the LORD,
for only he will release my feet
from the snare."

Though she had bounced back, and seemed to have leveled out, there was a short period again when she began crying.

When she couldn't explain at all what was troubling her, I raised the question of something unforgiven/unresolved, and reassured her that with our Yes to all that Jesus accomplished by his death for the world, even all our long-forgotten sins were covered. And if they pop up *in our minds* at some future date—like something up out of a deep black pond—those things already have been covered. Forgiven. Our grief at such unhappy recollections is justified; but we can be reminded at that point that "It's all been taken care of—it's covered. Be at peace."

As I went through all this with her, she was quiet; and the crying didn't recur.

(Talk time with her) This is further word from Psalm 25 that I have been sorting through.

Besides the things the Father has been rooting out of our lives, there are things that continue to trip us up. They are things we've faced in our lives, have asked forgiveness for, and have attempted to amend—knowing rightly that they keep us from walking in the fullness and peace that our Father has in mind for us.

But we can find ourselves still struggling with those issues, and too preoccupied with them. So, the psalmist has some wisdom for us. *Our eyes can be too much* on those things that trip us up, so that *that itself* is a part of the problem—still focusing on *us, on me*, and losing our hope. If I'm constantly looking "down" at what trips me up—obsessed with what is so frequently my trouble—far better to look *up, "eyes ever on Yahveh."* He is the only one who can release my feet from the snare.

As surely as we've lived long with each other, we've probably long known the issues the other struggles with—and have probably long been *praying for* each other about them. And God is good; He is faithful to love and embrace us even as we attempt to measure up to His Fatherly delight in us and purpose for us. (And He's faithful to honor our prayers for each other.)

Our hope, our encouragement, comes in the word that it's YOU, LORD, who *"release my feet from the snare,"* and that *"My hope comes from him."* (Psalm 62:5) Far better when you, LORD, are my obsession and not me myself and all my frailties.

> *O Savior. Thank you for our knowing about your saving love. It's you who've taken the initiative to make us yours, to win us, to own us; you who have the plan to refine us and complete us.*
>
> *Thank you for making us partners with you, in your passion to see us complete in Christ Jesus. Thank you for honoring our prayers for one another—in marriage, and in the Body of Christ.*
>
> *Thank you that we get to look at YOU, Jesus; YOU, the finished work that we're becoming.*

SOME THINGS MAY STILL GRIEVE A PERSON. THE BEST YOU'RE ABLE, REASSURE THEM—BUT WITH A REASSURANCE BASED ON THE WORD

Acts 3:21
Restoration of all things

*"...until the period of restoration of all things
about which God spoke by the mouth
of His holy prophets from ancient time."* (NASB)

Over those next months—in between dying episodes—her condition leveled out such that hospice had to keep re-evaluating to see that she still qualified. It was week-to-week of changes: of sleeping a great deal and then alertness, of eating or drinking well, then little—and finally then of being moved to that last corner of the dining section.

(With Elma) Old age and dying seems such a fruitless end to what's always seemed the exciting life of striving, coping, and achieving with the hope of accomplishing. And then *this: Aging,* and suddenly immobilized . . . and being dependent on other people. As you say, *"I's awfie to be awd and nae wan'ed*!"[22] It would seem to be just a bad joke, and tragic, if that's how life ended . . . If we didn't know that we are created to *live forever.*

But it's so good to know that this here—with all of the *sturm und drang* of this life—is our practice-ground, our training, our chance for learning . . . *how* to love . . . *to give . . . to forgive* . . . and to *die to ourselves.* To know that it's been a time to learn to trust the Unseen Hand. To experiment . . . and to come *to know and love* the God who has loved and engaged us to Himself through His Son.

Then, it's to realize and anticipate that *"there is coming a time for the restoration of everything!"* That what we've known and learned has its fulfillment. That bodies and minds, which have given us adventure and feeling and accomplishment and joy, will now be *restored to fullness.* That

---

[22] Scots dialect: *"It's awful to be old and not wanted!"*

the tentative relationship with the Unseen, which we have sensed from time to time, will be opened up to full wonder and joy.

O our God, thanks for all you've let us know and experience
of life, of getting to do and know and to love.

Thank you for the hope of our calling, the sharing in the
resurrection of Jesus—and for this from Peter—that there's to be
a Restoration of all that we'd begun to know here in life.

We praise you knowing that, as we've been able to love
and know here and now, we will get to love and know
and do, rejoicing in our life in you forever.

TALK ABOUT THE SEASON AS ALSO A PREPARATION FOR "THE TIME OF RESTORATION"

John 10:27-30
No one can snatch them

"My sheep listen to my voice;
I know them, and they follow me.
I give them eternal life,
and they shall never perish;
no one can snatch them out of my hand.
My Father, who has given them to me, is greater than all;
no one can snatch them out of my Father's hand.
I and the Father are one."

(As we talk together) John the Gospel writer was not a shepherd. He'd grown up in fishing. But it's not as though he knew nothing about flocks and shepherds; for they were everywhere in the Galilean countryside. And he'd have chased and played with sons of shepherds in the village market, and surely have known them in the *yeshivas*, where all the young were schooled under the local rabbi.[23] Then, too, of course, he'd have heard Jesus talk about "shepherds"—important figures forever in the mind of the prophets. And now in his own mind.

Everyone knew that "sheep know the voice of their shepherd" and won't follow the voice of a stranger. They also knew the reputation of a shepherd: that he'd die himself to save his sheep. Jesus had made clear that, to them, he was not only a rabbi with his students—but a *shepherd with his sheep*. And so, they looked to him not only for wisdom and insights, but for their life and destiny.

We're to do the same.

Jesus talks about "security" in a way that no other shepherd would dare or presume to talk: "*No one,*" he tells them, "*is ever going to be able to snatch you out of my hand.*" He underscores the guarantee: "*My Father who has given you to me—no one can ever snatch them out of HIS hand. My Father is greater than everybody.*" (Then, the clincher: "*My Father and I are one . . .*")

My love, we're in the grasp of Father and Son. No one can break us out of that grasp. And you know the song we sing:

> "*My life is in you . . . my strength is in you . . . my*
> *hope is in you: it's in you! it's in you!*"[24]

Father, our lives are hid in you with Christ Jesus. And when he (the One who is our Life) appears, we will also appear with him—in glory! Praise to you, Father and Son, forever—in your Holy Spirit! (Colossians 3:3-4)

---

[23] Dimont, Max I. Seventy-five years before Jesus' birth, a wife of one of the Hasmonean [Jewish] rulers in Palestine, Queen Alexandra—along with initiating vast social reforms—"*founded free elementary schools and made primary education compulsory for boys and girls.*" *Jews, God, and History* (New York, NY: Penguin Books, Ltd. 2nd Edition); originally published 1962; page 85.

[24] Words and music by Daniel Gardner. *The Celebration Hymnal*, p. 542.

Longing For Release & Home

2 Corinth. 4:16….5:2, 4
Meanwhile, we groan

"…outwardly we are wasting away,
yet inwardly we are being renewed day by day…
Meanwhile, we groan, longing to be clothed
with our heavenly dwelling.….For while we are in this tent,
we groan and are burdened…"

The restlessness for "home" was always there. It may have surfaced with cancellation of a particular "la-la" medication—in the spring before the October 4th crisis—causing the reality of her situation to emerge for her. Or, it could have been suggested with her hearing that she'd come under hospice.

Whatever, it reoccurred surprisingly, months later; and she began talking about "leaving" again. It came up with questions one evening at bedtime: "What do I need to do? . . . "What do I need to take with me?"

There was nothing else. Just that. But I'm caught off guard. So I fumble . . .

(Trying to keep it light.) What do you need *to take with you*?. . . (Chuckling, stalling trying to figure what she's thinking) . . . "Less and less" is the answer, I'm glad to say. (Then gradually getting ahold of it, I attempt the rest of this.)

Just have a look at us. We're continually leaving *more and more behind*. And you can guess that in God's plans there are a few more things for Him to do with us yet . . . But as for stuff that *we* need to do—*ourselves*, Sweetheart? We're pretty well near the finish line. (She's not laughing, but I'm trying to do so.) Seriously, we ourselves are getting ready to be with the Lord—chomping at the bit, I can say, for wanting to be with the Lord.

(Then I pull out this scripture.) Outwardly, the Apostle rightly says, we're wasting away . . . And that's surely true . . . But we're not to lose heart, he tells us, because inwardly we're *being made new* every day . . . That's important to realize, and I believe it . . . This "treasure" of the Lord Jesus *is in us* . . . and as all this stuff-of-living happens to us, the Apostle says, the life of Jesus is managing to break through *to be seen* in us . . . that's important! It's meant to happen that way.

Namely: as we go through all this—even this unwelcome, difficult, final Course of Aging stuff—Jesus' own life is breaking through *to be seen—in us!* . . . And, my Sweet Love, looking at you, I believe it is doing so . . .

At this point in the process, she was sleeping lots, eating and drinking little, often many days having little or no response. But the "leaving" comments continued over the next month: "It won't be long . . . Not for long. . . . I need to run away (sobs) . . . ." And with the sobs, I began to read to her further from the extended 2 Corinthians 4:7-5:10 passage, and to sing this song—many times:

"Oh, how He loves you and me. Oh, how He loves you and me.
He gave His life, what more could He give?

O, how He loves you. Oh, how He loves me.
Oh, how He loves you and me."[25]

Holy One of Israel, who was, and who is, and who is-to-come:
You who live forever, we bless you, we worship you . . . for loving
us . . . knowing us, purchasing us, and making us your own.

Hallelu-Yah, you who live forever!

BE READY TO TALK OPENLY ABOUT OUR LEAVING HERE

---

[25] *The Celebration Hymnal*, #349

Romans 8:29
Conforming to the Image

"…predestined to be conformed
to the likeness of his Son,
that he might be the firstborn
among many brothers and sisters."

From mid-summer on, though sleeping much of the time, she was talking a good deal—mostly with chopped off sentences and unrelated words. Sometimes in unintelligible words . . . "tongues of angels"?

Still, I continued reading to her in the evenings. And she listened intently, occasionally commenting appropriately!

Early a mid-October morning, in the apartment together, Elma turned to me, looked fully at me, and said distinctly, "HOW LONG . . .?" She didn't elaborate.

(Here's how I talked with her.) This one bears going over—then over again—when we're impatient with what's happening to us . . . impatient with the wait . . . with the hurting times . . . the helpless times . . . the confusing times . . . in the times when God seems to have hidden His face. This word from God tells me that more is happening than we can see, which He is working *on us*.

The *"conforming work."*

He's producing something in us as yet unseen . . . finishing the work of refining, maturing . . . putting to death the last of the stuff in us that's not worthy or ready for His Presence.

And He knows what He's doing; there's a template for it: it's "The Firstborn." We're being fashioned into his likeness. That's what the Father has in mind for us. And He hasn't forsaken us, nor has He forsaken the eternal plan and purpose for us. It is Life and Relationship with Him forever.

It's good to know that this is all not *"for nothing."*

It's also a good thing to know that He uses our prayers for each other in what He's doing. And it's good to have in mind, so we can be *more specific in how we pray for* each other—to know as you put up with those things that still aggravate you about me, for instance. (Mm-hm, you smile about that . . .) Because, really, those annoying reminders can be the things yet for which you cry out on my behalf.

Yes, and I know I may laugh as I talk about it . . . but it's serious business as we agonize on behalf of each other in the Body of Christ . . . before The Throne of the One who has in mind His beautiful but bloodied Firstborn—as the goal for our own lives.

I praise you, Father, for the beauty of this woman you've given me to love. I see the effect of your work in her, and it's wonderful to behold. How I love her! How I love YOU. How we together love and adore you, Sovereign Holy One.

We bless you for making your Son "flesh of our flesh, and bone of our bone" so that by his victory on the Cross you could complete in us what you've had in mind for us since the beginning of time.

LET THEM KNOW—REMIND THEM AGAIN—THAT GOD IS AT WORK IN US, DOING SOMETHING BEAUTIFUL

Revelation 5:9-10
A Kingdom of Priests

"…and with your blood you purchased men for God….
a kingdom and priests to serve our God,
and they will reign on the earth."

Happy times with family visits. (Ttt) Trying to talk. Joking and laughing.

(With Elma) O yes! God is not content only to *save us* . . . to make us right with Him and bring us to Heaven. But also, so importantly, He says about us that, *with his blood*—Jesus' blood, that is (it's serious business)—*Jesus purchased us out of every tribe and tongue . . .* in order to make us "*a kingdom and priests to serve our God.*"

There's a footnote: We're to "*reign on earth.*" We're saved, not just to wait it all out until death comes and whisks us off to heaven. O no! In the meantime He has every reason to use us as a "Kingdom of Priests" on behalf of the cultures and nations—which are, up to now, self-destructing and scheduled for Final Destruction. We're to be priests, who are to intervene on their behalf with prayer and radical lifestyle.

We're to do so, *with prayer that changes outcomes.* For nations, for individuals. In our history are all those stories of outcomes *changed* with prayer and fasting. Look at "Dunkirk": all those troops getting saved, under cover of overcast skies. And Kenya in 1963,[26] through prayer and fasting of a few hundred believers, bringing that nation to be an island of democracy in a surround of dictatorships.

And, as with my Dad, Yahveh our Father uses our pain and afflictions to focus our cry. Because of my Dad, you know, we've become assured that God uses our afflictions to bring requests to His Table—as together when you and I agree regarding the nations or the people on our own hearts.

> *Our Savior, what a wonder you are! Here we are, bed-bound and limping, failing in strength and sight, but important in your sight. You hear us and know us. And we offer our afflictions/ limitations for the building of your People—your covenanted People.*
>
> *Lift your pastors and teachers, the small-group leaders and catechists, your witnesses in all kinds of trying situations. Cover them with your Tenting Power, in Jesus's name.*

AS MUCH AS POSSIBLE, OPEN UP THE SCOPE OF THEIR LIVES WITH STORIES OF GOD'S AMAZING GRACE IN ANSWERING PRAYER

---

[26] Derek Prince, *Shaping History through Prayer and Fasting.* New Kensington, PA.: Whitaker House, 1973, 2002.

Psalm 139: 4
A word on my tongue

"Before a word is on my tongue
you, LORD, know it completely."

"I see a change in her this week," observed the Director of Nursing. Elma was eating little and hard to wake.

That same time, in the apartment, she awoke to look at me searchingly; so I said, "We're okay. We're going to be okay." She blinked her acknowledgement, then surprised me with a big smile and a teasing word: "I don't know about that."

The rest of the day she was mostly unresponsive. But in her room after supper, she gave a blink to my asking: "Do you want a story?" and reacted rightly to a sorry situation in a "Little House of the Prairie" episode. She then hung onto my narration of this Psalms reading.

(With Elma) *"Before a word is on my tongue,"* God knows it. That could be scary to hear, I know, but—when it comes to His knowing what is on our heart when we're praying—that's wonderful to hear, isn't it?

We've prayed together about a lot of things—the situations with our children and certain ones of our grandchildren. And God has honored our prayers so greatly over the years. And when I've had a lot of my projects and concerns, you've always been right there with me to hear me out and pray along with me. (You still do. I hear your "amens" yet, and I know you're with me.)

And it's so important that *you know* that God hears you still when you pray. This word tonight was so reassuring for me to hear, to know that *before a word is on your tongue, God knows it.* And to know that the things on your heart—even though these days *I'm having such trouble* hearing people, and even oftentimes strain and stretch to hear *you*—that God-in-His Spirit has no such difficulty hearing you. But that—even "before a word is on your tongue," Elma—He knows it.

And Romans 8:27 says that the one *"who searches our hearts knows the mind of the Spirit, because the Spirit intercedes for the saints—that's us—in accordance with God's will."*

His Spirit knows what's needed; and when you, Elma, sense those things in your spirit, and the word arises in your heart, He is so quick to pick up on it and do those saving things that He's intended.

But even more then: in moments that do come, when we're beyond praying—no word at all, and empty—Jesus speaks a word for us, he High Priest for us. In those moments, helpless on our own to cry out, it's so good to know that he is there to do so for us.

Thank you, God our Father, to hear that you know the cry of our hearts, even before the word is on our tongues. But, oh, so good also to know that the Lord Jesus, covering for us as High Priest, takes over in those times when we're beyond even praying for ourselves. O God our Father, we're so grateful to you. ¬Thanks for loving us and sealing us in your Forever Love. Guard over my Beloved this night, treasuring her in Christ Jesus.

WHILE THE PERSON STILL HAS SOME FOCUS AND ENERGY, LET THEM KNOW THAT GOD STILL HEARS THEIR PRAYER

Psalm 18:32-36
He enables me

"It is God who arms me with strength and makes my way secure. He makes my feet like the feet of a deer; he causes[27] me to stand on the heights...."

Our times were very limited by now. She was still coming with me each morning, but almost immediately after lunch she was in bed and asleep. So, it was mostly evenings that we had for talk time by then. And that was mainly with her in bed for the night, the room darkened and the small bedtime lamp on for me to read by.

Nightly I was telling her the many stories of her life, and she was

---

[27] An earlier version of NIV that I was using said: *He **enables** me to stand on the heights..."*

greatly attentive. I told tales of her and her iconic "Four Aunties," of each house we'd lived in, and of the birth stories of each of our children. It's the latter that prompted me to read from this Warrior Psalm 18 and to tell of this event. (As I told it, her eyes shone, her face intent and smiling as she relived the time with me.)

(With Elma) God enabled you. It was just weeks after the '67 Detroit uprising, and we'd been right in the middle of it as you know. Our third-born was all of eighteen days old. Mom and Dad had come to help in those first weeks post-partum and were on their way home that day by train. We'd driven them to Grand Central Station and were standing on the platform for our goodbyes, talking to them through the window, when you said, "Keith, there's something the matter with your Dad!" (He'd slumped in his seat where he'd sat while waving to us.)

You prompted me, "Get in there and see what you can do." I started into the train, which was still standing waiting to leave. Inside, I found Dad not breathing. I panicked as to what to do. In you came. You'd left our children outside, handed the baby to a middle-aged black lady (on the platform with her family seeing off friends) and coached me step-by-step in CPR . . . mouth on Dad's mouth, etc., . . . 'til finally, concluding Dad was gone, you urged me with the reminder that: "Hearing is the last to go. Talk to your Dad while he can still hear you." I spoke the crucial words into Dad's ear. "Dad, go in Christ Jesus." (I can't remember if I said any more or if I said I love you.)

Officials were coming by then, ambulance people. All happened quickly. They took over with the CPR, loaded Dad onto a stretcher and into an ambulance, shepherded me into the back with him and on and away to the Detroit General Hospital. You'd somehow gotten the children together, found the car in the parking lot, and pursued the screaming ambulance—with the black lady and her family following. (They found you and stayed around long enough until satisfied that they could do no more. We never knew their names; had no way to follow up on and thank them. "Angels . . . ?")

But God enabled you. And you enabled me, for what was a pivotal moment between my Dad and me. You always, my spectacular lady, rise to the occasion. Enabled by God to "stand on the heights" when I'm wobbling . . .

O Jesus, Warrior-God, son of the Father, thank you for how
you faithfully carry us through the moment. I praise you again

*for this remarkable lady, and for giving her to me, and for all
these years coming to love and enjoy and appreciate her.*

THE STORIES ARE INVALUABLE
FOR THEM AS WELL AS YOU

Hebrews 11:8-16
By faith, a City prepared

*"By faith, Abraham . . . obeyed and went, even though he did not know
where he was going . . . looking forward to the city . . . whose builder is
God . . . All these people . . . still living by faith when they died . . . God is
not ashamed to be called their God, for he has prepared a city for them."*

She's alert. (Ttt) Taking a ride to the parlor and the sunshine streaming
in. To my question, "Are you content?" I get a big smile. We hear music
on the stereo as I work on computer. There are kisses, talk, and (ttt). On
the patio we hear and see two mockingbirds. "Beautiful!" she comments.
Later, in her room, she is silent, distant. At bedtime she was fighting to
stay awake for our talk.

(With Elma) Abraham was "looking for a City." Funny, how all of
our life we have lived for *community*, lived *in community*, hungered *for*
community. We were nurtured in it in Scotland with devoted, eager,
earnest-but-struggling people, eager to bring the good news to an alienated
culture lost in the maze of industrialized slums. We tried to bring it about
in inner city Detroit. We introduced fervent, gung-ho friends to houses
where they might live nearby and help with the city's vast problems; and
only one, our former-nun friend, moved in to share life together.

Then coming to southern Indiana, there were the two couples who
wanted so badly to move along with us and be mission-community with
us. Both visited, but both found it impossible.

In Evansville, three other families tried to find a way with us to be a
community-in-mission together; but distance and other obstacles again

made it unworkable. So, in Scotland, in Detroit, in our two homes in Indiana, we've had *people, people, people, in and out of our home*. But the call to "faith-community "never quite materialized.

We've lived for the reality, longed for the reality. But it was always just out of our grasp. Yet, look—*how we have loved . . . how we have been loved!* We're absolutely *rich* in friends.

This Hebrews chapter is very much *our* chapter. The promises are very much our promises. We've seen things accomplished—and many things still painfully unrealized. But God is not ashamed to be called Our God, and He is holding the City for us where it all comes together.

God, faithful God! How we love you. How we love your King-dom. How we love it that you have made us for eternity, that you have made us for loving and being loved, and for living in Community —for eternity!

REMIND THEM: GOD HAS MADE US FOR ETERNITY.

BUT HE HAS ALSO MADE US FOR RELATIONSHIP.

John 14: 3
Jesus is the Way

"I am going there to prepare a place for you.…
And.…I will come back and take you to be with me
that you also may be where I am."

I woke with the sense that I was losing her today . . . .

At dinner she ate little. All day, she was silent, distant. In her room at bedtime, her kiss had a little taste of iodine. She was so low. So, I talked to her of "Jesus, the Way."

(With Elma) Tired? Yes, you're tired, and I know you are. It's okay . . . and it's so reassuring to know that "they've readied a room in the Father's House for us," and that vast expenditure in the preparations has been made for us by the Son. Jesus is getting us ready now for the journey . . . He knows the way . . . and he *is* the Way.

He's given us here a taste of LIFE and activity . . . But just a *taste . . .* for there's *more . . . much more ahead.*

We've given our acceptance to the invitation; with our Yes to all of the Son's preparations we've done so. Whenever in previous times we've been invited to some friends' house for dinner, you'd always look around for whatever hospitality gift we could bring. Well, this time, hospitality gift or no hospitality gift, *we are going!* . . . "*Nothing in my hands I bring; simply to the Cross I cling.*" This time, just to *lean back* and *rest . . .* On the Everlasting Arms . . . to be carried . . . totally *carried!*

(By this time, she was asleep.) I'll see you in the morning . . . and in the Morning of mornings! And then I sang:

> "*Finish then thy New Creation, pure and spotless let us be. Let us see thy great salvation perfectly restored in thee. Changed from glory into Glory, til in Heaven we take our place. Til we cast our crowns before thee, lost in wonder, love, and grace.*" [28]

REMIND THEM OF ETERNAL THINGS THEY KNOW . . . EVEN IF THEY HAVEN'T KNOWN THEM

---

[28] The Celebration Hymnal, verse 4, #648.

SONG:
"Steal Away to Jesus"[29]

"Steal away, steal away, steal away to Jesus.
Steal away, steal away home.
I ain't got long to stay here.
My Lord he calls me,
he calls me by the thunder.
The trumpet sounds within my soul:
I ain't got long to stay here."

She's sleeping lots. But when awake she's bright and happy. Many ttt's, but then so many cogent responses as well—as when I was getting ready for a funeral, to tell me: "You look very nice all dressed up."

Ate and drank little. In the evening, a clear desire for bed—*welcome bed!* Loving responses, verbal and vocal, kisses and eyes. (Such a sweet Good Night.)

(With Elma) I know there's a story behind this song. Apparently, spirituals, as used in the underground railroad by African-imported slaves, had a double meaning. On the surface, to sing about "stealing away to Jesus" meant dying and stealing away to heaven. But to slaves with a different intent, it also symbolized slipping away *to freedom.*[30]

For us now there's a kind of contentment in the song itself, in its simple lyrics and pentatonic melody. There's a reality in its words: *"I ain't got long to stay here."* It's not morbid to say so, but rather *a strength*—in knowing that the One in whom I'm abiding is the One to whom I'm going.

And once we've come to terms with that reality, the (at first "distant") sounding of the trumpet becomes rather welcome. Tired, and tired of life's dwindling days, its dwindling interests, I welcome hearing: *"I ain't got long to stay here."* I don't have to linger here forever! It's the Father, nicely calling us and starting to get us ready.

---

[29] Traditional Spiritual, public domain.
[30] "Pathways to Freedom." 2017 Maryland Public Television.

Thank you, Lord Jesus, Son of the Father! For loving us. For singing to us. For carrying us. "Anytime now," Lord Jesus, we're ready. Glory all the way.

Glory to You and the Father, in the Holy Spirit! We love you!

TALK ABOUT READINESS TO GO. IT'S OKAY TO HELP THEM LOOK FORWARD AND NOT TO BE AFRAID

Song:
"My Lord, What a Morning"[31]

> *"My Lord, what a morning . . .*
> *Be lookin' to my God's right hand*
> *when the stars begin to fall . . ."*

Though so tired, she was making efforts to talk, and to stay awake for stories, enjoying interviews on TV stations. She enjoyed our brief walks, including to a sunshiny parlor where she exclaimed, looking out the windows at the brightness of the morning, "Look at that. Isn't it beautiful!"

Her hands had been closed, claw-like, for months; and I'd made attempts with her to exercise thumb to finger, then to hold a fork and help it to her mouth. One evening at supper in her room she herself initiated the exercise. She'd joke—laughing at her attempts—and was making apt comments, "Never mind . . . Not necessarily."

(Our talk time) *What a morning!* And don't miss the pointer about "my God's right hand." For *there*—as it sings— there at the right hand of God is The LAMB! Slain for us. Changing history for us. Breaking the power of death for us. He, "the Son of Man"—his own term for himself, our substitute, our Representative Man—shining as the Glory we're to become, even as he embodied the Shame.

---

[31] Traditional Spiritual, public domain.

M'Love, there's coming a time (yes) for hearing "*the sinners shout . . . to wake the nations underground.*" We maybe won't hear it, because we won't be around when it happens. But it's good to know that it's coming. And to know it's not just because things have gotten so out of hand, and so tragic. But it's because, all along, the Father—He and the Lamb, together—have had the whole matter in their hands. His Bloodied Hands. All along.

Morning is coming! Tears "*may remain for the night—yes, we know—but rejoicing comes in the morning.*" (Psalm 30)

My Lord, what a morning . . . when the stars begin to fall . . . For, looking to my God's right hand . . . there you are, Jesus, Son of the Father, ruling, reigning, holding together in righteousness the whole of the Creation. For our sakes, bearing our sin, opening the way to The Father!

How we love you. How we adore you. Our rest is in you.

TALK ABOUT IT: MORNING IS COMING ! AND THE FATHER HAS THE MATTER IN HAND

LET THEM HEAR IT: THE SOLID, FUNDAMENTAL BASICS, THE THINGS OF THE ETERNAL HOPE.

Embracing The Big Plan Ahead

HYMN:
"Finish then thy New Creation"

> *"...pure and spotless let us be;*
> *Let us see thy great salvation perfectly restored in thee.*
> *Changed from glory into glory, till in heaven we take our place.*
> *Till we cast our crowns before thee,*
> *Lost in wonder, love and praise."[32]*

Days of fatigue followed. She was awake but tired, slumped again in her chair, looking very ragged. She smiled at mention of "the two little boys" (the youngest grandsons), and tried to take part (ttt). There was little response much of the day. Immediately asleep at bedtime.

The last day of October, she was deep asleep as I came for her to bring her to the apartment. She woke briefly to my kiss, but then was deep asleep again. After lunch, on the patio, she mostly slept again. Evening, again on the patio for supper, it was lovely, mild. She ate three bites. Then, TALK! "...pretty pink clouds"; and then more talk—so much so, that I gave up trying to remember and write it all down. She initiated hands play, she initiated a kiss. She was so fun that I did something I'd never done: I took a "selfie" of the two of us! She laughed and laughed, and said, "O, you're terrible!"

It was such a perfect evening. I said so, and she said, "That's what I was thinking."

It *WAS wonderful* . . . and *pen-ultimate,* in a way that neither of us realized . . .

---

[32] "Love Divine, All Loves Excelling" by Charles Wesley. The Celebration Hymnal, #648.

*(With her asleep) O Beautiful Creator, what a wonder you are!
The plans you have for us. The glory you've created us for. The
things you've been doing amongst us. There is none like YOU.*

*And I praise you for giving me this remarkable Lady! I love to
tell her so, Lord, and I love to tell you! You're so good. Thanks
for teaching us to LOVE—the greatest gift to my life!*

YOU HAVE NO IDEA WHAT TO EXPECT. BE THERE

2 Peter 3: 10 - 13
A Day promised

*"...the day of the Lord will come like a thief...
live ... as you look forward to the day of God
and speed its coming ...
in keeping with his promise,
we are looking forward to
a new heaven and a new earth,
where righteousness dwells."*

Three days later . . . . in the evening after our supper, as we were
waiting in her room for the CNAs to come—out of nowhere, she said,
"NEXT WEEK!" A big knowing smile on her face.

(With Elma) God's got a Day! There've been a lot of big days. But
with this one, there'll be the fulfillment of everything for which Heaven
and Earth were created in the first place. All the beauty, the wonder, the
marvel of Creation, the exhilaration of life and of the purpose for which
everything was made: it all has its culmination in what the Sovereign, Most
Holy is going to do when He has His "Day of Days."

And we get to be in on it: we get to celebrate with it. We're part of what
He's been doing and planning and working all these aeons. He's created
us to know Him, to love Him, to serve Him.

The angels will get to celebrate what we've become: and what we are even now, in Him. And we will get to celebrate Him and the glory and wonder of His Son's accomplishment for us: the amazing wonder enabling us to live forever and to be what He's created us to be.

There'll be a Feast. Oh, yes. And a Wedding. We don't understand even half of it. (We don't have to. But we're in it.) And it's for us. But it's all about the Lamb and the New Day.

And finally, everything will be *JUST RIGHT.*

> *"O that will be Glory for me. Glory for me. Glory for me.*
> *When by his grace I shall look on his Face:*
> *that will be Glory, be Glory, for me."[33]*

ANTICIPATE. LOOK AHEAD. RELISH THE TIMES YOU HAVE. RELISH THE MOMENTS.

Hebrews 11:32- 12:1
The Great Cloud

> *"God had planned something better for us*
> *so that* only together with us *would*
> *they be made perfect.[34]*
> *Therefore, since we are surrounded*
> *by such a great cloud of witnesses . . ."*

She was tired, sometimes not looking good. But she was wanting to stay awake, trying to talk (ttt), and getting out some words—"KEITH" with a shout one day and a big smile. Big smile along with "face-hugs."

With word of a coming visit from a son, she queried, "….Jennifer and the others?" Then there was a great effort to talk as she watched me

---

[33] Glory Song, by Charles H. Gabriel. The Celebration Hymnal, #769.
[34] Better than "perfect": being brought to completion, finished. From the Greek word, *telei-o-tho-sin* (RSV-Interlinear Greek-English New Testament.)

folding laundry. In one of those talkative efforts (phrases which I couldn't understand), she joked at what she had said. And laughed and laughed.

On one evening, seeing she was weary of the TV, I asked if I should I turn it off and read instead. With her consent I did so, and she said clearly (with a knowing smile): "You're good."

She was still vocalizing response to our prayers; and as I told stories of our escapades, she'd confirm details I'd ask about and, though tired, rise up to be there. And, always, kiss responses.

But she was tired.

(With Elma) There are a lot of folks waiting for us. And not only waiting; they have a stake in our finishing well; *their own completion* is wonderfully, amazingly tied up along with *our* completion. For the Apostle states clearly that "only together with us" will they be *brought-to-completion*. Interesting isn't it, that we are so wrapped up together in our destiny? It's no wonder the stands are cheering for us (I picture a great stadium, jammed with people—us, on the playing field, they in the stands). They're celebrating the victory of our God, of course; but besides that, they're cheering (interceding?) for us who are still in the warfare.

If our part in the warfare *seems* insignificant, it's not insignificant at all. Our "warfare" in this Final Season is to wait on and trust God. And as we continue to do so, He's been doing that quiet finishing work in us which is so important: *"conforming us to the image of The First-Born"!* (Rom. 8:29)

Oh, don't let anybody disparage what God is doing in the unwelcome thing we call "old age"—or try to shorten or curtail it. You, Elma, are a shining example of it: you've always been beautiful, but God has been doing a *beautiful thing* in you; and it is such a joy to me, and to others, to see it.

O LORD our God, wonderfully guard over our sleep, wake us in the Morning of Mornings to see your face. We love you, we're so grateful to you.

CELEBRATE THE BIG PICTURE OF WHAT GOD IS DOING, NOT ONLY OF WHAT'S AWAITING, BUT THE GOODNESS OF HIS PRESENCE EVEN NOW

Psalm 73:25-26.
The Promises

"Whom have I in heaven but you?
And earth has nothing I desire besides you.
My flesh and my heart may fail,
but God is the strength of my heart
and my portion forever."

This one is on the wall, above Elma's bed and above mine—with instructions: "To be read to me when I can no longer read it for myself."

She was tired. Eating almost nothing. Drinking very little.

The Indianapolis families each came down for a quick visit the week before Thanksgiving. She was so tired. Her usual rising to respond to them was so weak. Slept. If awake, mostly quiet. Big quiet smiles in the corridor for staff. And still vocalizing with me at prayers some nights.

And then a very strange response which I'm still uncertain how to explain. Our daughter had already returned home. It was while our younger son was still here that it happened: she gave a high little scream—almost a yelp! (It startled us.) It was just a little scream, but cut off so quickly that "a yip / yelp" is the only way I can describe it. She'd been asleep. There had been no seeming response from her until—with that little yip—there was a look at Jonathan, a little glimmer of recognition for him.

Was it a desperate attempt to say, "I'm here. And I know you're here . . . ?"

It happened again the two succeeding days after Jonathan had gone. And again, a fourth time, three days later.

That last time was a day alone with her for me.

(With Elma) I guess it's not unusual. We didn't pay much attention to The Promises during all the years of active life. We knew the promises: that we're made for eternity . . . that Jesus has gone before us . . . that he's prepared a place for us . . . that there's a great cloud of witnesses cheering for us . . . that there's to be a new Heaven and a new Earth . . . that we'll be in The Holy One's presence to praise Him and rejoice in Him forever.

But while we were involved and active, relatively healthy and relatively "in charge"—O dear, how relative it all is—there wasn't much point being overly obsessed with the end of life. Or eternity. It must have been different, a generation or so earlier, before we thought healthcare and hospitals could take care of everything. And different too, certainly, in third world countries where average lifespan is much shorter, and an accident or an illness could end life in a moment . . .

> *But now, O Loving Father, how quickly we've come to know for ourselves that "my flesh and my heart may fail." So, thank you for knowing that you, God, are the strength of my heart. And you're our portions forever! Thank you that you've taught us to trust you in the times before, and that we can trust you in this Final Time as well. Give us peaceful rest tonight, and rejoicing in the morning*

STAY. LISTEN. KEEP LOVING THEM WITH THE WORD OF GOD, AND THE WORD OF YOUR LOVE

2 Cor. 1:19
Amen to all the promises

> *"Jesus Christ…preached among you*
> *…was not 'Yes' and 'No',*
> *but in him it has always*
> *been 'Yes'."*

Three days later was a day with almost no responses except the little scream ("I'm here. And I know you're here.") Apart from that, she was asleep, slumped, and when awake totally quiet. No food. No response.

No kiss responses—until that evening.

At bedtime I told her the story of our leaving New Harmony and of our thousand friends and the Luke 16 story of "being welcomed into Eternal Homes." At our Good Night she looked at me to give me her three blinks ("I love you"). And a kiss.

(With Elma) What a faithful God He is, Our Shepherd, to carry us forever! He has carried us *so far!* He has brought us through *so much!* Then, what a word this is from the Apostle Paul: that, with all of the promises, revealed to the world by the prophets and the apostles—*they all have their "Yes and Amen" in Christ Jesus!*

And, we're heir to those promises.

Elma, I am so grateful for this time we've had. It's been hard—Oh, yes—but I wouldn't have wanted to lose *any of it.* A sweet loving time in which God has ripened our love for each other. Funny, funny times we've enjoyed. Quiet, deep times. Not just the times on the patio, watching skies and clouds; the hawks and squirrels, the birds—the remarkable presence of the two mocking birds on that recent morning. But it's been the stories retold and relished . . . the times of napping, of watching and waking to see one another . . . to see each other, to love, to hold, and cherish each other.

In your promises, Faithful God, you have gifted us with life and love and eternal life.

Thank you for loving us, and for teaching us to love. I praise you for the gift of this woman: apart from your promises, Lord—the greatest gift of all of my life.

With everything you've given us, Savior, we look forward to the fulfillment of it all in the Morning of Mornings.

TELL THEM HOW PRECIOUS THEY ARE TO YOU, EVEN AS YOU LET GO AND HELP THEM LET GO

SONG:
"Be glory for me!"

"O that will be: Glory for me! Glory for me! Glory for me!
When by his grace I shall look on his Face:
that will be Glory! Be Glory for me!"[35]

Thanksgiving Day.

Elma had slept through breakfast time in the dining room. Why have they even brought her to table at this late date? (They bedded her down at my request.) Midmorning, briefly, she woke. I sang songs with her.

At noon when they tried to feed her, food dribbled out of her mouth. She had no motivation for it. She was looking unwell, grey.

At supper, Elma accepted a bit of water. I read Derek Prince stories. Elma fell asleep as I prayed. ("I'll see you in the morning.")

(With Elma) *Thank you, O our Father. O God, how I*
love her. I praise you for her. I commit her to you.

"O that will be Glory for me! Glory for me! Glory for me!
When by your grace we shall look on your Face:
that will be Glory! Be Glory for me!"

TALK IN THEIR EAR. QUIETLY SAY THE THINGS OF THE VICTORY, OF THE ANTICIPATION, OF THE REALITY

USE WORDS OF SCRIPTURE, OF SONGS, OF YOUR OWN LOVE

---

[35] Glory Song by Charles H. Gabriel. The Celebration Hymnal, #769.

Psalm 118:15-16
Shouts of joy and victory

"Shouts of joy and victory
resound in the tents of the righteous:
'The LORD's right hand has done mighty things,
The LORD's right hand is lifted high...'"

The Friday after Thanksgiving Day.

Elma is asleep. Nurses have left her in bed. No food or drink all day.

Family arrives late in the day for our usual, post-Thanksgiving, Friday-Saturday celebration. They're all here, variously in and out of the room, talking. The smallest grandsons and their dad are playing cards on the floor. There's no attempt for a meal together; they've all had the big meal. There's no particular hush. Elma sleeps right through with very little response. It's a normal family gathering time, the perfect setting for Elma in her deep sleep.

Then, as Saturday morning of the holiday comes, and it's time to go home, there is a bit of hesitation. There's the usual talk of starting back for work on Monday. But should they?

At 11:30 a CNA changes Elma and we notice her breathing pattern changes. She's begun a rapid, labored breathing. Hospice is called. But still there's the indecision: "Elma has done this before." She could continue like this for two more weeks, they tell us. So, the families reluctantly begin their goodbyes, and leave.

Delight, relief, for all you brought us through, our Savior. Hyped
by the victory song, we're so rejoiced at the victory and the presence
and the testimony. Can't wait til it's all culminated in your
Coming . . . . or in our coming to you! So, get those Gates ready. When
you're ready, God-of-our-Salvation, we are. We love you, Lord.

WAIT. CONSOLE. ASSURE.

"IT COULD BE DAYS YET." BUT IT MAY NOT BE.

WAITING. WATCHING. LOVING.

Psalm 118: 15, 18-19.
Open for Me the Gates

*"Shouts of joy and victory resound
in the tents of the righteous . . .
The LORD has chastened me severely,
but he has not given me over to death.
Open for me the gates of the righteous;
I will enter and give thanks
to the LORD."*

I have my supper on a tray beside her. Then I sing some of our songs to her—sometimes sitting by her, sometimes leaning over close to her face.

*"O how he loves you and me,
O how he loves you and me.
He gave his life; what more could he give:
O how he loves you, O how he loves me,
O how he loves you and me."*[36]

I read and talk scripture to her, particularly these last verses from this Psalm 118. While I'm reading, our daughter phones. She's back home. I put the phone up to Elma's ear; and Jennifer talks to her, loving her, letting her go. I see no response in her face.

The weekend hospice nurse who comes in (one we don't know) urges me to go back to my apartment and get some sleep: "This could go on a few more days." So, I finish my prayers with Elma, kiss her good night, and at 7:00 go to my room. I fall asleep okay.

At 2:00 the night nurse wakens me. "Elma is gone."

I dress and go my usual trip down the corridor to see her. To see her, and hug her (still warm)—those little, sweet "face-hugs" in bed we'd do—and to find myself, mid-hug, just pouring out *thanksgivings* and *hallelujahs*, as if it were the most natural thing in the world to do . . . remembering she'd told me so many important times that "the hearing is the last to go" . . .

---

[36] Celebration Hymnal, #349.

So, I talk, believing she hears it as I sing, and as I tell her how I love her . . .

O LORD, we'll not die, but live, and proclaim what you've done. You've chastened us severely, but not given us over to death; So open for us the gates of the righteous. We'll enter in and give thanks to you, LORD."

"You've removed my sackcloth, and clothed me with joy." (Psalm 30:11

"You saved me because you delighted in me." (Psalm 18:19)

THE HEARING IS THE LAST TO GO

TELL THEM THE LAST, LOVING, ASSURING THINGS FOR THEM TO HEAR

As a young woman, 19 or 20, looking out the window
of her summer cottage on the Island of Iona

In the dressing room on her wedding day

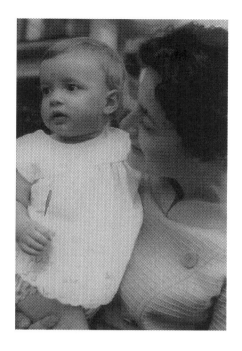

As a young mother, with daughter Jennifer

In her prime, enjoying relationships with her young mothers

With Keith, in a teasing moment

Mid-years, with Keith

Beaming. Still finding joy in a gifted contentment

An Afterword Moving Into Another "Sea"

After Elma's death, in the weeks after the burial, I fully expected to die. With any one of my frequent angina episodes I was having, I didn't bother to take nitro pills. I just waited, expecting too to die. It wasn't that I withdrew from life. I continued to go to meals, to write, to visit the skilled nursing area, to play an occasional card game. I continued to meet with people both in my apartment and in going out for meals.

But I didn't expect to live, and I didn't want to live. I resisted the thought that there might be another "season." I balked at planning ahead. I'd already lived out the Final Season with Elma. It was done and I saw nothing more to welcome of life or of days. I not only didn't want to live—I resented living. I acknowledged to God that I was willing to finish whatever work there was but then expected Him to "Let me go, please."

Meanwhile, I slogged through the days without relish—until gradually I realized there was a bad taste in my mouth. It occurred to me that I was being rebellious . . . willful. Unfaithful? . . . I didn't like the thought. But it kept bugging me. Even as it was so apparent, the remedy was so unwelcome: I needed to repent. (Repent? Why repent?) God was giving me length of days and I was refusing to honor it; I wasn't accepting continued days as gift, or as further assignment.

Reluctantly I apologized to the Father, the Sovereign, the Holy One— King of kings and Lord of lords. The Boss. My Friend. The One who loves me. And reluctantly I asked for help: "Help me to embrace it—even though it's a new and unwelcome season, without Elma."

(A new season?) What that means is still hard to fathom. I'd been reading a book by a navy admiral about the major oceans and seas. With maps—which I always enjoy—he wrote of the narrow straits that lead from one major body of water to another, as the Straits of Malacca leading from the Indian Ocean to the China Sea.[37]

That gives a picture of my now life. I've just come through difficult straits and am now in a new . . . . call it *"Sea"* instead of season. These last three months since the anniversary of Elma's death have been the hardest, with illness morphing into depression. But with her safely on the Other Side and confident I'll see her again, I'm trying to navigate this further strange Sea with its unknown swells and shoals.

I no longer drive. In The Home, this aging-center where I live, relationships are tentative; for staff and residents come and go. So, with waning health—and despite multiple activities—people keep mostly to themselves and do their best to contend with loneliness and uselessness. But that is the sphere of my call now: to know, to love and encourage the other "little afflicted brothers and sisters" like myself nearby—that, as well as the wider sphere of many friends and family in my life outside and in the creative world of the internet . . . All of which will continue, of course, only as long as "parts work" and I'm able to function.

Meanwhile, I find that the same things I helped Elma navigate, I myself have to navigate. All the things I sang and said with her, I need now to claim and know for myself—until The Glory opens up and Jesus carries *me* to that not-so-distant Other Shore. Then, O . . .

". . . that will be Glory for me,
Glory for me, Glory for me.
when by His grace I shall look on His Face:
that will be Glory, be Glory for me."

REASONS FOR WRITING

Certainly, Sister Genevieve started it. I had no intention of writing about what I was in the midst of—the turbulence of the previous three or so years. But a few months into hospice care, this same Genevieve, as hospice

---

[37] The Straits of Malacca, a narrow, 550 mile stretch of water which runs between them, has long been a threat to ship owners and the mariners who ply them.

chaplain, began telling me of the needs of other people going through such a time. Not only that, but she was telling me that I (apparently) was doing something right with Elma; for she began saying to me, "Keith, you need to *write!*" (Genevieve can be very commanding.) "People need to know this."

In that first year's time with Elma in nursing facilities, I saw the film, *Tsunami*, with its scenes of trauma and devastation and separation, of those tumultuous waves, of being swamped, pulled under tons of water and gasping for air. I told friends I hadn't needed to see the movie: I'd been living in a Tsunami.

To keep my own head above water, early on I began to take notes of our odyssey. I had had enough experiences by then to realize the need to be very heads-up, because institutions themselves can lead you a merry chase and leave you swamped. It's not only the ill person wondering "What's happening," but you—the supposed one-in-control.

So, I took notes of my times with Elma, mornings, afternoons, and evenings. Of her condition: her moods, her responses, the events around us. Eventually, her words. By the time she was in hospice, I had already been noting all these things. It became an important reference for the weekly visits of the hospice nurse.

In the early months after her death, I began by writing down all the verses and songs I'd used with her. And I soon realized that whatever I would have to say all revolved around those meditation times. So, from there, reading and high-lighting the episodes in my journal, I began to write—what I could remember of how I used each scripture or song in talking with her.

It was wonderful for me. And now that I've come to the anniversary of her death, I am so grateful for getting to review and write about those times, getting to relive them as I wrote. I call it "an odyssey," and a "love story," because that's what it's become for me.

As for all of you reading this: Every experience of dementia is surely different; and ours may be scarcely applicable to yours. Yet, it may possibly be a help as others look ahead and see themselves aging . . . and as (with some foreboding) they begin to move into their own "pen-ultimate" times . . . or anticipate the possible need to care for one another . . .

Besides Sister Genevieve, others encouraging me have been Cindy Ragsdale and David and Liz McFadzean. They, together with Beth Storms and daughter Jennifer, were the ones most helpful and challenging. Any glaring faults are mine for when I didn't heed their advice.

Keith Hueftle, March 27, 2018.

If you feel like writing me, please do so. My email address is:

keith@ke-huper.net

Printed in the United States
by Baker & Taylor Publisher Services